THE COMING RUSSIAN INVASION OF ISRAEL

Thomas S. McCall
and
Zola Levitt

moody press
chicago

To
our beloved wives,
Carolyn McCall
and
Yvonne Levitt

© 1974 by
THE MOODY BIBLE INSTITUTE
OF CHICAGO

ISBN: 0-8024-1607-1

Paperback Edition, 1976

14 15 16 17 Printing/LC/Year 87 86 85 84

Printed in the United States of America

Contents

CHAPTER   PAGE

Foreword   5

Preface   6

Introduction   7

1. The Russians Are Coming   9

2. The 4,000-Year Tragedy: Ezekiel the Prophet   15

3. Brinkmanship: Ezekiel the Political Analyst   25

4. From Russia with Blood: The Invasion of Israel   40

5. Satan on the Battlefield: The Armageddon   51

6. "Thy Kingdom Come"   65

7. A Strategy for Christians   80

8. A Strategy for Unbelievers   88

3

Foreword

WE'RE LIVING in electrifying days of fulfillment of ancient Biblical prophecies. At just the time that the predicted King of the North is making obvious moves toward securing a foothold in the Middle East, and that whole part of the world has become the focal point of all nations, this clear and timely exposition of Ezekiel 38 and 39 setting forth *Russia* as this King of the North couldn't be more relevant. I feel this book is a must for everyone who wants to know where we are on God's time-table.

HAL LINDSEY

Preface

THE WORLD TODAY is like a bomb with a lighted fuse. Conditions everywhere indicate that it is only a matter of time before the bomb is ignited and a global upheaval takes place.

The Coming Russian Invasion of Israel is a warning of the approaching explosion. Like a man who sees flames enveloping a building and cries, "Fire!" the authors sound an alarm.

It will not be surprising, then, that many will regard the authors as alarmists. In a sense of course, that is exactly what they are. But when there is a real danger (and there is!), anyone in his right mind appreciates being warned.

In the pages of this book there is not one note of false alarm. The coming catastrophe outlined is real. It is based upon that which is declared by God Himself in His eternal Word.

Biblical prophecy sets forth the future of Russia with dramatic clarity. Her invasion of Israel at the end of this age is incisively predicted in the Bible as clearly as the regathering of the Jews and their establishment as a present-day nation in Palestine.

This treatise on prophecy, though popularly written, constitutes a reliable guide to what is going to happen in the world in the near future. It will benefit everyone who reads it. The Christian will be strengthened in his faith in God's Word. The non-Christian will see his need of Christ's salvation to prepare him to face impending world catastrophe.

MERRILL F. UNGER

Introduction

THIS BOOK has been exceedingly difficult to write, because the events the authors intended to "predict" kept virtually coming to pass during the writing.

The authors are not the prophets, of course, but Ezekiel and the other Bible writers who foresaw the coming Russian invasion of Israel have become so timely that it is difficult to set down interpretations of their prophecies before the events actually happen.

When we began this project in the summer of 1972, the idea of Russia invading Israel was a matter of the future, though many recognized it as a possibility. But in the fall of 1973, during the writing, the Yom Kippur War broke out in the Middle East, and the American military went on "Alert," apparently fearing a Russian invasion of the combat area.

When the authors speculated, in 1972, that the oil of the Middle East might become a vital issue of world affairs, we didn't dream we would be waiting in line for gasoline in Texas a year later!

This book is more than timely. We feel that it is a grim necessity to warn the world, believers and unbelievers alike, that the biblical messages about today's world affairs are relevant and imminent. The coming Russian invasion of Israel is not far off, and it will profoundly affect us all.

Since 1948, when Israel was revitalized, the Arab world, Europe, and the superpowers have all been engaged in an escalating confrontation about the Jewish state. Russia has emerged as the major enemy of Israel over the time. We believe, with Ezekiel, that Russia's animosity will not be satisfied short of an invasion.

While this particular development has surprised the world, it comes as no surprise at all to students of the Bible. For twenty-six hundred years, the Russian invasion of Israel in the end times has been common knowledge to readers of Ezekiel.

As with our first book, *Satan in the Sanctuary,* we have taken a single issue of Bible prophecy and have attempted to illuminate it completely in the light of current events. This time we have had to constantly revise the manuscript to keep up with ongoing developments. We felt, at times, that we might be too late. This may yet prove to be true.

But if you have this book in your hands before the Russian invasion of Israel, please know that the alarms sounded here are real. Ezekiel and the other prophets have been right too many times for the world to ignore them any longer.

And this issue is serious. It is truly a matter of life and death.

As we watch the coming Russian invasion of Israel in preparation, we pray that many thousands of readers will put their trust in the true Author of prophecy, the Lord Jesus Christ, and that believers in Christ will redouble their efforts to tell the redeeming Word of God while there is still time.

Until the coming Russian invasion of Israel, "The truth shall make you free" (John 8:32).

T. S. McCall
Zola Levitt

1

The Russians Are Coming

RUSSIA IS going to attack Israel.

If we had said it a few years back, it would have been a perfectly impossible idea, the way things stood.

But the prophet Ezekiel said it 2600 years ago.

Ezekiel 36 to 39, which we will examine in detail, is one of the Bible's "histories of the future." It chronicles, by means of symbolic visions given to the ancient prophet, the coming Russo-Israeli war. It discusses the actual battle campaigns and the outcome, as seen by the war correspondent Ezekiel.

This is not to be confused with Armageddon, the "war to end all wars." The Bible also foresees that ultimate conflict, but the Russo-Israeli war is to precede it.

Ezekiel places his prophecy in the End Times. The Bible continually refers to this final period of earthly history when God's plan for our world will culminate. It will not be a happy time. It is commonly called the Great Tribulation. And it seems to be coming up very soon.

Biblical descriptions of the end times include a host of issues quite familiar to readers of today's newspapers. Jesus, whose second coming is to climax the tribulation period, warned His disciples about the strife and tension, false prophets, famines, earthquakes, and national conflicts which have now become the world's daily bread. He said, "Nation shall rise against nation," and He told of "wars and rumors of wars" (Matthew 24).

There is not adequate space here to consider all the prophecies about the end times and apply them to our world situation.[1] Suffice it to say here that the world today has all the requirements to satisfy Ezekiel's gruesome visions of the Russo-Israeli war, and mankind's most comprehensive achievement of self-destruction, Armageddon.

Past ages could not hold a candle to us for weaponry, attitude, and the general know-how of destroying one another. The world has always had war, but our thermonuclear capabilities, international tension, and disregard for human life make us the best contenders ever for the honor of receiving the One who said sadly, "Except that the Lord had shortened those days, no flesh should be saved" (Mark 13:20).

If there is to be global war, we are the ones who can do it.

But first, the Russians are coming.

Ezekiel sees a massive land invasion from the far north into the Middle East. The Scriptures urge upon us that Russia will be the nation to mobilize an enormous land army which will cross the Caucasus Mountains, Turkey, Syria, and Lebanon, to attack Israel. It's David and Goliath again, and again a question of the faithful against the pagans.

And again God takes quite an interest in the affair and sides with the underdog.

1. Hal Lindsey, *The Late Great Planet Earth* (Grand Rapids: Zondervan, 1970), and Thomas McCall and Zola Levitt, *Satan in the Sanctuary* (Chicago: Moody, 1973) give more complete discussions of end-time prophecies.

The outcome of the war is given: Russia meets her Waterloo. "I am against thee, O Gog," says God. "Thou shalt fall upon the mountains of Israel, thou, and all thy bands, and the people that is with thee: I will give thee unto the ravenous birds of every sort, and to the beasts of the field to be devoured. Thou shalt fall upon the open field: for I have spoken it, saith the Lord God" (Ezekiel 39:1, 4-5).

The concept of a huge land army vanquished upon the open field is still very much a part of our modern warfare, automated as it is. We are going to discuss Russia's rationale for a march to Israel and the unique circumstances that will come about to satisfy the prophecy.

THE SICKLE AND THE SCIMITAR

For Ezekiel, to foresee an alliance between Russia and the Middle Eastern nations was going out on a limb. The pagan Middle East was, in his time, a most advanced civilization, the world's center of scientific knowledge and refinement of culture. It had dominated the Mediterranean for a period longer than from Christ to the present. Its magnificent architecture, religions, and military might were acknowledged and respected throughout the civilized world. But Russia, so far as anybody knew, was inhabited by roving bands of virtual cave people.

But just look at how things are now. Russia is a tremendous power. The claws of the bear have reached out in all directions from that vast frozen land, and Ezekiel is getting more believable by the day.[2]

The Arabs have become mere middlemen now as Russia

2. For further information, see *Russia, Imperial Power in the Middle East* (Jerusalem: Carta, 1971).

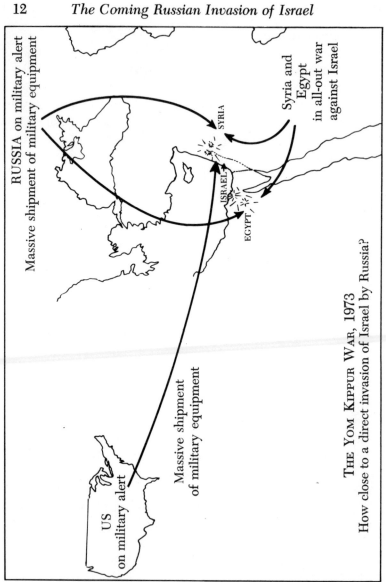

THE YOM KIPPUR WAR, 1973
How close to a direct invasion of Israel by Russia?

advances upon the true cradle of civilization, the Holy Land.

In late October 1973 the American military went on "Alert" in an announced response to Russian troop movements. It was said that Russia was planning to move combat troops into the theatres of the Yom Kippur War. Some said the maneuver was purely a political gambit, but the important thing was that nobody was really surprised. For Russia to attack Israel would not be at all out of line with current developments.

That's never been true before in history. Until our present days, nobody except Ezekiel ever thought that Russia would attack the Holy Land.

But in the past twenty-five years, Russia has increasingly become Israel's arch-enemy. She has armed the Arabs. There has been an enormous outlay of men and material for war steadily flowing to the Arabs from the Soviets, and it amounts to one of the most fearsome military mobilizations in history. Along with the death machines come talented Russian technicians to teach modern vengeance to the Arabs, who have no lack of vengeance in their own right.

Some of those Arab soldiers put on their first pair of boots one week and learn to use a rocket launcher the next. But the knowledge and the equipment keep piling up.

ISRAEL SEES RED

Israel does not regard the Arabs as the real enemy, wisely enough. When you're shot with a Russian-made AK 47, you might as well give credit where it is due.

General Moshe Dayan, hero of the 1967 Six-Day War, has stated flatly, "Israel is now at war with Russia."

The Arabs have their much-touted reasons to fight—they claim that the Jews took their land, they don't belong there, and so on. But the real issue here is Communism, the irresistible force of world atheism, against Judaism, the cradle of belief in God.

That is how Ezekiel saw things. Through him God named the real combatants—the enemies of God versus the friends of God.

2

The 4,000-Year Tragedy: Ezekiel the Prophet

THE CROWDS must have really come out when Ezekiel held forth. His was a rare kind of ministry. He was a walking, talking example of national tragedy, demonstrating by his own sufferings what was to befall the nation of Israel. God told the Jews, "Ezekiel is unto you a sign: according to all that he hath done shall ye do" (Ezekiel 24:24).

It was a tough assignment. Patient Ezekiel, thought by some to be insane, endured an unrelenting series of personal tragedies and afflictions. He was a one-man show—a living drama of disaster.[1]

He shut himself up in his home, bound himself, and was struck dumb. He was ordered by the Lord to lie on his right side for 390 days, and then on his left side for 40 more days, by way of demonstrating to Israel the number of years of her iniquity.

His food and water were rationed by God, and he was charged to eat disgustingly unclean bread. "Thou shalt bake it with dung that cometh out of a man" (4:12). He lost his wife but was not permitted even the consolation of mourning.

1. See Charles Lee Feinberg, *The Prophecy of Ezekiel* (Chicago: Moody), p. 224.

And that wasn't the half of it.

His suffering still goes on, in a way, because his majestic book is probably the least known and least heeded of the Bible prophecy books. With all of his painful efforts, his messages seemed largely lost on the ancient Jews, and on us too.

It's time to give this unsung hero his due. We're about to see the fulfillment of his boldest, most dramatic visions reenacted by whole nations rather than by one lone man of God.

He was one of the prophets of the Exile, the period when the majority of the Jewish nation was detained in Babylon in the sixth century B.C. King Nebuchadnezzar of Babylon had taken his place somewhere in the middle of the list of those tyrants of history with solutions to "the Jewish problem." He had laid siege to Jerusalem, examined his prisoners—an entire civilized nation—and simply carried off all but the poor and indigent.

In the bargain, he acquired some of God's key men. Ezekiel and the brilliant Daniel were among the captives. Jeremiah, whose clear-eyed forecast of this very disaster proved accurate to the letter, was left behind with those not worth deporting.

We can gather that the Jews were permitted to function within their traditions while detained, since the prophets went about their work. From the confines of ancient Babylon, Daniel and Ezekiel were able to see events of our own times and beyond. It is fair to say that they were able to see the end of the world as we know it.

Ezekiel's visions confounded his audiences, and they still leave the casual reader mystified. But as world events progress, we have the advantage of seeing the pieces fall into place. It would have been a lot to ask of the unhappy prisoners of Nebuchadnezzar to picture a mighty Russian army swarming down on Israel. But this is not nearly so hard to picture nowadays. Ezekiel is rapidly coming into fashion.

He begins his story of what we are calling the Russo-Israeli War with a typically bewildering vision of a valley filled with dried bones. God takes Ezekiel into this grisly scene to make a point. The prophet describes his conversation with God:

> And He said unto me, Son of man, can these bones live? And I answered, O Lord GOD, thou knowest (37:3).

You can't blame him for hedging. Ezekiel must have been as baffled as we are.

God orders Ezekiel to speak to the bones—to say to them, "O ye dry bones, hear the word of the LORD" (v. 4).

Some preachers today complain about speaking to "dead" audiences!

Ezekiel did as he was told, prophesying to the dead bones that they would live, that God would restore them with new sinews, flesh, skin, and breath.

The situation has been immortalized in the spiritual "Dry Bones." "Dem bones gonna walk aroun'," says the likable tune accurately enough. Ezekiel reports, "I prophesied as he commanded me, and the breath came into them, and they lived, and stood up upon their feet, an exceeding great army" (v. 10).

The meaning of the vision is revealed by God in the ensuing passages:

> Then He said unto me, Son of man, these bones are the whole house of Israel: behold they say, Our bones are

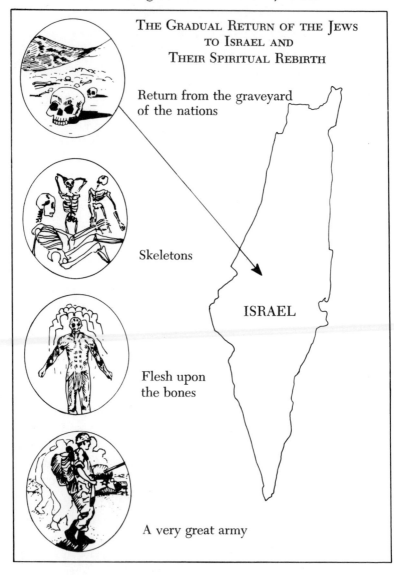

THE GRADUAL RETURN OF THE JEWS
TO ISRAEL AND
THEIR SPIRITUAL REBIRTH

Return from the graveyard
of the nations

Skeletons

Flesh upon
the bones

A very great army

ISRAEL

dried, and our hope is lost. . . . Therefore prophesy and say unto them, Thus saith the Lord GOD; Behold O my people, I will open your graves, and cause you to come up out of your graves, and bring you into the land of Israel (vv. 11-12).

The vision teaches the regathering of the Jews back to Israel from the "graveyards" of the Gentile nations.

This part of the prophecy is easy enough to understand for anyone living after A.D. 1948 when the Jews truly were regathered to their promised land. It wasn't quite as easy to appreciate for those living in the long nineteen centuries between the destruction of the second temple of Jerusalem (A.D. 70) and 1948, when the Jews were dispersed and without a homeland.

To put Ezekiel and the end times into perspective, we should say something about the four thousand-year tragedy that is the history of the Jews.

The Jews have had a special destiny since the day God made His covenant with Abraham (Genesis 12). They became for all time the Chosen People. This status, though ultimately a profound blessing and privilege, has had its ups and downs. Because of the Jews' very special responsibility to God, they have constantly enjoyed, or suffered, divine interest in their affairs.

This is not just a theological viewpoint. History bears out the distinctive joys and deep despairs of this chosen people.

Tevye, the poignantly Jewish protagonist of *Fiddler on the Roof,* cajoles God, "Why don't You choose somebody else for awhile?" A look at the story of Judaism explains his discouragement.

The Jewish nation, as a political entity, really begins

with the enslavement in Egypt. With the great exodus from slavery led by Moses about 1500 B.C., the Jews were given a land promised by God. There followed almost a thousand years of autonomy peace and the building of an intellectually and scientifically enlightened civilization in Israel.

The high point of that reverent and politically successful millennium was the middle of it, when the Jewish nation progressed to world importance under the leadership of David and Solomon. The brilliant King Solomon achieved the great ideal of God and the Jewish people when he constructed the magnificent Temple of Jerusalem.

There followed, however, a decline in the Jews' reverence for God. The prophets constantly warned the people —God had full charge of this nation and would act according to its faith.

Speaking in worldly terms, pagans to the north were gaining strength and military skills, and the Jews, relaxed in their now well-established and successfully defended kingdom, failed to heed the signs of the times.

When the prophet Jeremiah frantically sounded the alarm—actually naming Nebuchadnezzar of Babylon and the Chaldees as the near-future invaders—the government was unimpressed. In fact they were so annoyed that they jailed the prophet to quiet his clamorings.

About the only individual who thought Jeremiah had something to say was Daniel, who faithfully studied the older master's conclusions about the predicted Babylonian exile. God gave Daniel the incredible prophecy of the seventy weeks, in which he foresaw the advents of the reclaiming of Israel, the first coming of the Messiah, our own times, and even the future return of Christ.

Ezekiel was at this time carrying out his own difficult assignment among the captives, and looking ahead to the far-future Russo-Israeli war.

The Jews were released from Babylon by the conquering Cyrus of Persia, as prophesied by Isaiah and Jeremiah, and once again they put their amazing nation-building powers to work.

By 516 B.C. they had established the second Temple in Jerusalem, and they proceeded through a shaky five centuries as a passive little country coexisting with Persia, Greece, and Rome.

They held on while Alexander the Great and numberless other pagan conquerors traded the known world back and forth, until the times of the Roman Empire.

Rome had a Russia-like knack of gathering territory, either quietly or with the sword, and a bottomless appetite for taxes. By the time of Christ, the Jews were exceedingly uncomfortable with their divided loyalties—their faith went to God, but their worldly produce went to Rome. They plotted rebellion.

This was a very bad idea. In a worldly way, they had no chance whatsoever in a war against Rome; spiritually they were in a state of extreme disobedience to God—they had rejected their Messiah.

They got together a national rebellion just after the time of Christ, in A.D. 66, and Rome dealt with it unmercifully. In the final siege of Jerusalem and the battle for the Temple site, the Jews suffered more than a million casualties in five months!

Only Hitler could rival such easy accumulation of Jewish bodies. The Jewish nation took more losses in that final campaign than the United States has suffered in all of her wars since 1776.

But the unkindest cut of all was the destruction of the Second Temple. The Romans were so thorough that Jesus' prophecy was completely fulfilled: not one stone was left upon another.

But the depleted little nation staggered on. It's very hard to picture what a society is like when one out of every three people formerly functioning is dead. But the Jews somehow pulled their society back together and went on, heavily taxed and strictly policed by their Roman masters.

By the time of the emperor Hadrian, about A.D. 130, they were thinking rebellion again. There had been several skirmishes through the years, with heavy Jewish losses, and war on a national scale was in the offing. Hadrian provoked the Jews by building a pagan temple on the Jerusalem temple site and forbidding or restricting many of the Jewish religious practices. He gave the Jews credit for Christianity—a charge they hardly appreciated. He was clearly trying to obliterate the very idea of Judaism, and he almost succeeded.

This war in A.D. 135 was actually a guerrilla operation in which the Jews fought like the Viet Cong; they spread the rebellion out over the whole of the country, picking at the Romans with endless small campaigns and ambushes. The enemy obliged with a nationwide mop-up.

The Jews were plainly too difficult to rule; the tedium of constant policing, the recurring combat, and the detested monotheism steadily emanating from Jerusalem finally tired the Romans, and they threw the Jews out of the land.

Thus began the great dispersion of the Jews that lasted until 1948.

There are no times of joy to report from that long period. Somehow the Jews, still faithful to their religious practices wherever they happened to be, never could get themselves back together. From the days of Christ on, the Jews have had steady heartbreak.

The whole world now became the enemies of Judaism. Somehow no one could let the vanquished Jews just rest. They were slaughtered like animals during the Inquisition. They were starved and murdered endlessly in forced conversions throughout Europe. Persecution followed them to the ends of the earth.

Russia was no exception. The Jews suffered terrible pogroms and conversion-by-starvation. The present Soviet restrictions on Jewish emigration continue the tradition.

And finally the peerless Hitler came forward to attempt the complete extermination of the Jews.

This, at last, gave the world a bad conscience about the Chosen People, and they were once again permitted their promised land.

The events since 1948 are within memory and show little slackening of the typical troubles for the Jews. The Arabs are following in the footsteps of the cruel Egyptians of antiquity; the Russians are getting up steam like Babylon did.

Now we turn to prophecy to know the future of Israel. Ezekiel will take us on from here.

From surveying Jewish history, we can better appreciate how much meaning there is in this "dry bones" vision of Ezekiel. "Can these bones live?" Can a people dispersed without a common culture for all those centuries ever pull themselves together again? Can dead things come back out of graves and be restored to their ancient land?

Only by an act of God.

> And ye shall know that I am the Lord, when I have opened your graves, O my people, and brought you up out of your graves, And shall put my spirit in you, and ye shall live, and I shall place you in your own land:
>
> then shall ye know that I the Lord have spoken it, and performed it, saith the Lord (37:13-14).

3

Brinkmanship: Ezekiel the Political Analyst

HERE COMES THE PART we were telling you about.

Ezekiel now analyzes the coming Russian invasion of Israel. Chapter 38 introduces "Gog, the land of Magog, the chief prince of Meshech and Tubal" (v. 2), and says of them "Thou shalt ascend and come like a storm, thou shalt be like a cloud to cover the land, thou, and all thy bands, and many people with thee. . . . And thou shalt come from thy place out of the north parts . . . a mighty army" (vv. 9, 15).

The names "Gog" and "Magog" are a bit cryptic, but it is not difficult to trace just who is meant here. Serious students of the Bible had identified Russia with these names long before she achieved her present supremacy.

The new Scofield reference edition of the Bible states, "The reference is to the powers in the north of Europe, headed by Russia . . . the attempt to exterminate the remnant of Israel in Jerusalem."[1]

It is fascinating to compare the note to this passage found in the old Scofield Bible, annotated in 1909—in the Czarist age of Russia. The brilliant commentator C. I.

1. *New Scofield Reference Bible* (New York: Oxford, 1967), pp. 881-82, note.

Scofield could not have foreseen either the rise of Russia to world importance, nor the regathering of the Jews to Israel in 1948, but he says, "That the primary reference is to the northern (European) powers, headed up by Russia, all agree. . . . The reference to Meshech and Tubal (Moscow and Tobolsk) is a clear mark of identification. Russia and the northern powers have been the latest persecutors of dispersed Israel."[2] Scofield's reasoning has been kept intact in the latest edition, with only the deletion of the word "dispersed."

The genealogy of biblical names is a study in itself, and beyond our scope here. *The Late Great Planet Earth* gives a clear background in the chapter "Russia is a Gog," pointing out that the terms of Ezekiel 38 first appear in Genesis 10.[3] They are actually names of sons and descendants of Noah, and it was the custom for tribal, and finally national, names to evolve from original founders' names. Apparently the tribal name Magog moved northward from the Middle East. Josephus, a Romanized Jewish historian of the first century, notes that Magog is called the Scythians by the Greeks. Secular history books trace the fierce Scythian people, who lived in the northern regions above the Caucasus Mountains, as forerunners of modern Russia.

But even without all of that, we can still clearly see the Bear of Russia through the geographical hints given by Ezekiel. He stresses three times over that this mighty enemy of Israel comes from the "uttermost north" (38:6, 15; 39:2). The original Hebrew gives the qualified meaning "extreme" or "uttermost" to the term "north" all three times. And of course, the ultimate power to Israel's utter-

2. *Scofield Reference Bible* (New York: Oxford, 1909), p. 883, note, Scofield's parens.
3. Hal Lindsey, *The Late Great Planet Earth*, p. 63.

most north is Russia, the nation most likely to succeed in being "a cloud to cover the land."

Furthermore, we have "Gog" identified as the "chief prince" of the invaders. The Hebrew phrase translated "chief prince" is *nesi rosh*. The word *rosh* can be an adjective meaning "head" or "first," but it could just as easily be a place name "Rosh." The Hebrew lexicon of Brown, Driver, and Briggs indicates that Rosh here is the proper name of a people.[4] It seems that Ezekiel's Rosh has become today's Russia. This is more than a hint! God indeed stands at the door and knocks!

And lastly, we have Meshech and Tubal, compared by Scofield and many others to Moscow and Tobolsk, militarily industrialized citadels of the future enemy. Moscow, as a matter of fact, lies due north of Jerusalem.

Russia by herself would be sufficient as an enemy, or, as the Jews sing on Passover, *"Dayenu!"* (enough for us). But Ezekiel specifies that there will be some allies on top of it.

Persia, Ethiopia, and Libya are given, clearly enough, and also Gomer and Togarmah (38:5-6). The latter two pertain to eastern Europe (iron curtain countries) and southern Russia, respectively, as we shall see. The former names have come down to us intact except for Persia, which is now Iran.

Curiously, Egypt is not mentioned among the antagonists. Will something happen to Israel's perennial enemy before the conflict? Will she not be important enough to merit listing among the allies at that time? Will the name Libya automatically include Egypt by then?

Persia, or Iran, would make a first-rate ally for Russia

4. Francis Brown, S. R. Driver, and Charles A. Briggs, *A Hebrew and English Lexicon of the Old Testament* (Oxford: Clarendon, 1959), p. 912.

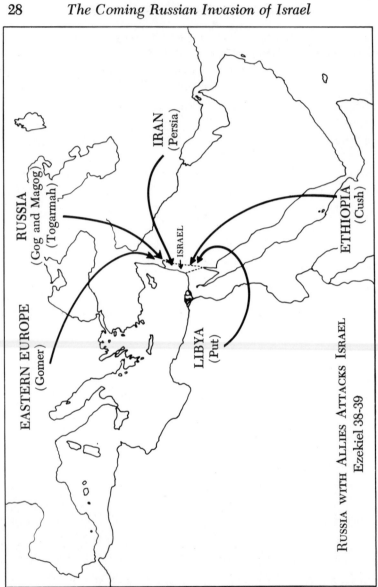

RUSSIA (Gog and Magog) (Togarmah)

EASTERN EUROPE (Gomer)

IRAN (Persia)

ETHIOPIA (Cush)

LIBYA (Put)

ISRAEL

RUSSIA WITH ALLIES ATTACKS ISRAEL.
Ezekiel 38-39

in a land invasion of Israel. Its location and terrain would greatly facilitate troop movements. Given the large scale of the invasion foreseen by Ezekiel, the mountain ranges separating Russia from the Holy Land become a factor; and those in Iran are more hospitable than those in Turkey.

The Elburz mountain range in Iran is not so extensive as the Caucasus in Turkey. The rest of Iran is generally more accommodating than hilly Turkey, too. And the advancing Russians could create something of a pincer effect if they arrived from two directions against Israel.

Ethiopia may represent more than the country that bears its name. Its ancestry is traced to Cush, a grandson of Noah (Genesis 10), whose descendants apparently migrated southward into all parts of Africa. The Organization of African Unity, founded 1963 in Addis Ababa, Ethiopia, was described by Ethiopian Emperor Haile Selassie as "a single African organization through which Africa's single voice may be heard."[5]

Libya's role is becoming more of a typecasting every day. It is easy to see that this advancing Arab power would be most receptive to participating in hostilities against Israel. It has ever been a nation typical of the Arab mentality and way of life, and it is presently arming. Giving some idea of how Libya is pressuring Ethiopia to work against Israel, a 1973 *Time* magazine report of a recent summit meeting of the Organization of African Unity says,

> Potentially the most divisive was a demand by Libya's Muammar Gaddafi for an all-out condemnation of Israel, and a break in relations by every O.A.U. state. Ethiopia and 26 Black African countries maintain diplomatic ties

5. "Decade of Destiny," *Time,* June 11, 1973, p. 44.

with Israel; Lybia, the O.A.U.'s five other Arab members and seven Black African nations are violently anti-Israeli.[6]

Gomer "and all his bands," is a reference to the countries of the Soviet bloc in Eastern Europe. Northward migrators who settled along the Danube and Rhine rivers, Gomer's descendants are traced through the ancient Cimmerians back to Genesis 10.

Togarmah is a reference to the area of Southern Russia or Armenia, and adds an interesting note to the method of invasion. The area is the origin of the Cossacks and is well known for its fine horsemen and its cultivation of superior cavalry forces. Ezekiel pictures horses being used in this invasion (38:15), and this very issue has been used many times to try to invalidate the prophecy. After all, who's going to ride a horse into a mechanized twentieth century battle?

These critics were silenced during the Korean War when the Red Chinese, no mean horsemen themselves, moved huge numbers of troops in mountainous terrain by this tried and true method. The invasion of Israel involves mountainous terrain.

In any case, these last two allies, Gomer and Togarmah, complete the picture of the invading force. Israel is virtually surrounded. The Mediterranean Sea is at the west of the Holy Land, and the invading allies will come from the north, south, and east.

It makes so neat a geopolitical picture of a logical coming invasion that it is almost too perfect. Perhaps we cheated a little, looking at the current scene and bending the prophecy to fit it?

6. Ibid.

Actually, the placement of the allies was researched and decided by Bible students long before the iron curtain takeover of eastern Europe, before the independence of Israel, before the rise of Russian Communism, and even before the alliance of distant nations was considered militarily feasible.

The Hebrew lexicon of Wilhelm Gesenius, written in the early 1800's, gives an analysis from which we do not differ.[7] Imagine what the scoffers thought back then!

THE CURRENT SCENE

We should go around the protagonists once more with a view to what they are doing on the current scene. Students of Ezekiel have never had a better opportunity to appreciate his foresight, and time may be running out.

First, Israel. Ezekiel beautifully pictures modern Israel with a few pointed remarks. He talks about the inner mountains of Israel "which have been always waste" (38: 8). True enough, until the present era, Israel's fruitful mountains were constantly desecrated by foreign occupiers. The Muslims dammed up the rivers of the lush Sharon Valley and made it a marshland in order to deter invasion. The forests of the little country, always dependable, were destroyed by occupying Turks, who unfeelingly cut down the magnificent cedars to build temporary structures.

The "land of milk and honey" was made almost into a desert.

King Solomon maintained a building program that was the envy of the ancient world, with largely domestic ma-

---

7. William Gesenius, *A Hebrew and English Lexicon of the Old Testament,* trans. Edward Robinson (Boston: Crocker & Brewster, 1854).

terials. But when the Jews got back their land in 1948, they had to first plant trees and restore natural irrigation in order to have wood. "Plant a tree in Israel" was the worldwide plea of the Jews in the 1950's, as school children sent their dimes to the Holy Land to restore it.

But a few verses later, Ezekiel pictures an improved land:

> And thou [Gog] shalt say, I will go up to the land of unwalled villages; I will go to them that are at rest, that dwell safely. . . . To take a spoil, and to take a prey; to turn thine hand upon the desolate places that are now inhabited, and upon the people that are gathered out of the nations, which have gotten cattle and goods, that dwell in the midst of the land . . . to carry away silver and gold, to take away cattle and goods, to take a great spoil (38:11-13).

This was quite a mouthful in Ezekiel's time. Who had ever heard of a land of unwalled villages back then? A wall to those ancient reckoners was what we call national defense today. The image shows how futuristic was the thinking of the prophet. And then we see that the invader, when he gets to "the desolate places that are now inhabited," will fall upon a people "that are gathered out of the nations." That must also have sounded strange to Ezekiel's audience; the Jews were not nomads, to say the least. Since they had a promised land, emigration was virtually a sacrilege. True, they were detained in Babylon because of military invasion, but Israel was still Israel. For the Jews to leave their land was to turn their backs on God. How could the prophet even speak of Jews as being gathered out of other nations?

Only an Ezekiel or a Daniel or an Isaiah—those possessed with the secret information given by God—could begin to picture the extent of Israel's coming exile.

Finally, in his statements about what the invader will encounter, Ezekiel depicts a successful nation, where the people "have gotten cattle and goods," and where silver and gold are there for the capturing.

What do these things symbolize? What does Israel have today that Russia would want?

Well, first there is very real wealth in Israel. The country is small, but enjoys a vigorous economy. The people have a Japanese-like enthusiasm that continually makes something out of nothing.

Then there is wealth in terms of raw materials. Little oil has been found there, but the mineral deposits of the Dead Sea, persistently defying extraction, represent a great prize. There is a wealth of brains too. Russia gobbled up tremendous amounts of scientific and industrial know-how when she took over in eastern Europe, particularly in East Germany.

We must keep in mind that invasions are not what they once were. When, for example, Nebuchadnezzar or the Assyrians accomplished an invasion, it was hard to tell a country had been there when they started. The new look in takeovers is much more discreet. The invading country attempts to leave intact all that might be useful to it—factories, farms, universities, laboratories—and have it all functioning on the invader's behalf. Ideally, the invader would like to just run up his flag on the flagpoles and leave everything else as it is.

The Russians are the masters here. Occasionally they

have "used the teeth on a knot that would not yield to the tongue," but they have by and large taken over vast amounts of the world with great discretion. Eastern Europe still functions; it just works for the Reds now. Where ideology would not work, they have employed tanks, but in any case the countries and their people end up second-class Russians.

Israel is a fine target for this kind of thing. She's the prize of the Middle East.

And finally, perhaps most importantly, Israel has a prime location for the orderly spread of Communism.

It is said that three things are important in real estate—location, location, and location. This applies whether you are buying the real estate or stealing it. Israel's location is of prime importance to Russia.

Looking on the world globe, one can see that Communism has enjoyed a steady, organized expansion emanating from Russia. It has gone to the Pacific on the east, the Berlin wall on the west, and to the frontier of the ice on the north. To the southeast it has penetrated Indochina with some difficulty. To the southwest—Israel's direction—it has jumped over some territory and penetrated in Africa and the Middle East. Israel stands right in the jumped-over spot.

Israel represents an outpost of democracy standing smack in the way of the communist expansion. She would provide a most convenient base from which the Communists could operate in the Middle East and Africa. She has good access by land and sea to these areas. Her harbors and airfields are among the best. The liability of the long supply line that has frustrated invaders from Alexander to Napoleon to Hitler would be eliminated in this sector if Russia could control Israel.

Ultimately, the oil of the Middle East might go to the great power close enough to grab it. The recent oil embargo proved how effective an economic and political weapon oil can be!

We have seen Russia establish outposts and then proceed from them to control vast territories. The situations in the Balkan and Ural countries led ultimately to the takeover of Eastern Europe. Operations from North Korea and North Vietnam were more troublesome, but cost the free world dearly to contain them.

A foothold in Israel for the Russians would obviously mean real trouble for everybody else.

Ezekiel's view of the spoils available seems conservative in view of the present scene.

Looking at the allies of Russia in the coming conflict, we can see that Ezekiel's stage is not completely set as yet—at least not at this writing.

Iran is not officially aligned with Russia at the moment, though such an alliance in the future would not be surprising. Ethiopia is not aligned with Russia either.

Libya is another matter. Recently she acquired fifty Mirage fighter jets from France, and she is learning how to use them (by trial and error). She has become an influential power with Egypt; indeed she may well supersede Egypt by the time of the invasion. Talk of a merger between the two nations is constant.

Libya's increasing importance in the Arab bloc, along with the fading of Egypt, may account for the lack of mention of Egypt in the prophecy. There has been a shift recently to Libyan predominance in that sector. While Ezekiel's listeners could have easily understood the participation of Egypt in an invasion of Israel, he omitted her and mentioned Libya. Will Egypt decrease as a major power among the Arabs by the time of the invasion? Will Libya be the key antagonist from that sector?

The northern allies are already dressed for their roles. Gomer (eastern Europe) can certainly be counted on by Russia to act on cue. Togarmah is literally part of Russia and may justify Ezekiel's unique picture of a horse-soldier invasion.

When will the invasion come?

Well, we cannot know, even with today's insights, the times and seasons of the Father, taught Jesus, but we can watch the signs of the times and interpret them. We mentioned some of the signs of our times which qualify this present generation to be the one living in the End Times, or "the latter days." This term, utilized by Ezekiel in this prophecy (38:8, 16) was also used by Jesus in His message about wars and rumors of wars. It is fair to say that all of our various circumstances might repeat together in some future time. But we would be remiss not to recognize the high correlation between the prophecy of Ezekiel and others, and the characteristics of our age.

Historically, few people ever really took the prophets seriously. This was a very bad habit we should now break. With the restoration of Israel and the rise to world importance of Russia, Ezekiel's once-confusing messages take on a new urgency.

We have looked at the details of the Russian alliance and the present scene. Before we go on, we might do well to briefly review the last twenty-five years of relations between Russia, the Arabs, and Israel. Are these nations really setting up for a major conflict at this time? Could Ezekiel have meant our generation? What about God's view? Israel is His chosen people.

In God's view, taught Ezekiel, this coming conflict is really a war between the atheists and the godly. The Arabs, sons of Ishmael and Muhammad, are virtually godless in the biblical view, while the Russians are outspokenly atheistic. The Jews, however far from their Messiah, are the worshipers of God in this conflict, and will be able to count on His promises, in the prophet's view.

During the last twenty-five years we have seen an ever-growing antagonism between the citadels of atheism and the promised land. When Israel was restored to the Jews, it brought up a feud that goes back four thousand years to the dispute between Isaac and Ishmael. The divine blessings and vast real estate holdings of their father Abraham were in question then.

They still are.

For nineteen centuries things were quiet between Jews and Arabs, while the Jews were dispersed throughout the world and the Arabs came and went as they pleased in Palestine. But Semites have long memories. When the Jews returned twenty-five years ago, they considered that they were getting back their land—the land promised to them by God.

The Arabs considered Israel (Palestine) to be their own ancestrally given property.

They might have worked something out, but Russia, hovering over the argument like a spectator at a prize fight, preferred the hostile atmosphere.

For her part, Russia at first thought Israel might be some sort of socialistic outpost in the Middle East, and she recognized the new state diplomatically in 1948. The original Israeli leaders, veterans of the kibbutzim—which resemble the Russian collective farms in some ways—seemed to embrace certain socialist concepts. But it was quickly seen by Russia that the new country was to be nothing like the materialistic, atheistic homeland of Communism.

The honeymoon ended very soon. Israel set up a kind of socialism which allowed for enormous concern for the individual human life, strong ties with theistic convictions and the Jewish heritage, capitalistic enterprise, and great political diversity. This was plain obnoxious to Russia.

Fissures appeared steadily in the relations between the two countries, until it was clear that the Russians preferred the company of the Arabs in the Middle East.

Three actual wars occurred, in 1956, 1967, and 1973, with Russia fully allied with the Arabs. Some propaganda about Russia helping the Arabs recover their cherished land was published each time, but the pretenses have cleared up now. It's now plainly a matter of land-grabbing and the spread of Communism.

The wars helped show Russia and the world that the new little nation was no patsy. The Jews were reminded of the great days of King David, when invading armies confronted Israel only at their extreme peril. The war of 1967 demonstrated Israel as a power to be reckoned with. The world looked on in astonishment as the Jews vanquished the Russian-armed Arabs in just six days.

There is now relentless rhetoric about renewed hostilities, and fickle Russia still waits on the sidelines, armed to the teeth and making alliances. She looks very much like she's just picking her moment.

These last twenty-five years argue very forcefully for Ezekiel's predictions coming out very soon. He gave no inkling of a lengthy period of brinkmanship, but gave his analysis of the invasion in quick chronological sequence after the restoring of the Jews to their land.

Due to the strange dramatic manifestations of God's word by the prophet, some people thought he was crazy. But he does not look crazy now.

Look now with Ezekiel at the actual Russian invasion of Israel.

4

From Russia with Blood: The Invasion of Israel

EZEKIEL: WAR CORRESPONDENT

"I AM AGAINST THEE, O Gog," says the Lord at the beginning of Ezekiel 39. "I will turn thee back and leave but the sixth part of thee."

In this stirring section, the prophet depicts in vivid detail the defeat of the mighty invader of the north and the terrible results of the war. "The sixth part" seems to refer to those spared of the vanquished Russian land force; this 84 percent casualty rate is unheard of in modern warfare.

It is hard to understand this severe defeat except as an act of God, which is what Ezekiel says it is. It accomplishes the purpose of glorifying God before Israel and the world, and of finally restoring much-chastened Israel to its God.

Interesting details of the combat and its aftermath are revealed in this chapter. Some have raised controversies of interpretation, but the overall picture is distressingly clear.

Apparently Russia is overwhelmed early in her campaign, virtually at the moment of the invasion. We see no lengthy scenes of battle, and the attackers will "fall upon the mountains" and "fall upon the open field." The invasion does not appear to affect population centers, and we hear of no destruction of Israel (39:4-5). Shades of the Six-Day War!

We are given only a hint of this supernatural conquering of a militarily superior force. Ezekiel quotes God, "I will smite thy bow out of thy left hand, and will cause thine arrows to fall out of thy right hand. . . . And I will send a fire on Magog" (vv. 3, 6). The allies of the invader are disposed of as well! "Thou [Gog] shalt fall . . . and all thy bands, and the people that is with thee" (v. 4).

The fire falling upon a land army is not nearly as difficult to imagine in this age as it was in Ezekiel's time. Napalm or even nuclear detonations might well be described in this way. But this is a matter of speculation. In the preceding chapter, Ezekiel supplied more details, quoting the Lord: "I will rain upon him [Gog], and upon his bands, and upon the many people that are with him, an overflowing rain, and great hailstones, fire, and brimstone (38:22).

Walvoord says, "Some natural questions are raised about this. Some have suggested that the description of hailstones, fire and brimstone might be Ezekiel's way of describing modern warfare, such as atomic warfare. There is a possibility that Ezekiel was using terms he knew to describe a future situation for which he did not have a vocabulary. The language of Scripture indicates, however, that the victory over this invading horde is something that God does. It is God, Himself, who is destroying the army."[1]

Ezekiel goes into quite a bit of detail about the aftermath of the war. Enough is left for scavenging birds and

1. John Walvoord, *The Nations in Prophecy* (Grand Rapids: Zondervan, 1967), p. 113.

animals; "I will give thee unto the ravenous birds of every sort, and to the beasts of the field to be devoured" (39:4). The dead bodies of the invaders apparently will strew the fields and mountains of the holy land, "And seven months shall the house of Israel be burying of them, that they may cleanse the land" (v. 12).

This lengthy burial detail will occupy a lot of people: "Yea, all the people of the land shall bury them" (v. 13), and some will find full-time employment at it: "And they shall sever out men of continual employment, passing through the land to bury . . . those that remain upon the face of the earth, to cleanse it" (v. 14).

With typical Israeli civic pride and endeavor, they will sterilize their promised land. Even travelers through the land—tourists—are to be asked to watch for stray remains, and to mark the spot for the burial details: "And the passengers that pass through the land, when any seeth a man's bone, then shall he set up a sign by it, till the buriers have buried it in the valley of Hamon-gog" (v. 15). "Hamon-gog" is the Hebrew for "The multitude of Gog," which is to become the name of this vast cemetery for the invaders.

This grim and morbid information about the burial emphasizes the very large size of the invading force and the totality of their defeat. But even more of a testimony to this will be the burning of the weapons that fall from the hands of the combatants. Ezekiel specifies that seven years will be involved in the burning of the weapons of this vast army.

"And they that dwell in the cities of Israel shall go forth, and shall set on fire and burn the weapons . . . and they shall burn them with fire seven years" (v. 9). This has a practical side: "So that they shall take no wood out of the

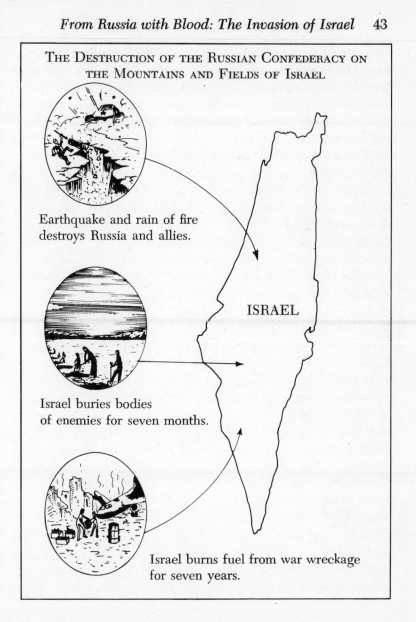

THE DESTRUCTION OF THE RUSSIAN CONFEDERACY ON
THE MOUNTAINS AND FIELDS OF ISRAEL

Earthquake and rain of fire
destroys Russia and allies.

ISRAEL

Israel buries bodies
of enemies for seven months.

Israel burns fuel from war wreckage
for seven years.

field, neither cut down any out of the forests; for they shall burn the weapons with fire: and they shall spoil those that spoiled them, and rob those that robbed them, said the Lord GOD" (v. 10).

So the trees of Israel, so lovingly planted one by one, are to be spared, while the weapons of the pillager are used for firewood. It all fits with the frugal, spartan ways of the native Israeli.

It fits, too, with the Israeli tradition of commemorating any struggle for the holy land. Today in Israel one sees 1948-model trucks and armored weapons—vehicles of every kind—still standing at the sites of their final battles. The Israelies leave them by the sides of the roads to remind the people how difficult this land was to attain. A French-built Renault tank stands in the brush at the southern tip of the Sea of Galilee, blasted into submission by a Molotov cocktail. It commemorates the successful defense of unarmed Daganya Kibbutz against a column of twenty-six Syrian tanks in the 1948 war of independence.

It would be fitting indeed for the Israelis to watch a seven-year memorial fire symbolizing still another defense of the promised land.

But how can they burn tanks, trucks, and armored vehicles? How can the weapons of modern conflict be destroyed by fire?

On this point there is still much controversy. Ezekiel's descriptions are in keeping with his time and his own vocabulary. He speaks of burning "the shields and the bucklers, the bows and the arrows, and the handstaves, and the spears" (39:9).

His readers and listeners could well understand these terms, though they could not understand the presence of

Russia. We can understand the presence of Russia, but have some trouble picturing them invading with archaic weaponry.

Some think Ezekiel's weapons are symbolic representations of the weapons of modern warfare. Perhaps, for example, the reference to the invader coming "like a cloud to cover the land" (38:16) describes air warfare in the language of the sixth century B.C. Bows and arrows might be launchers and rockets. Spears might be rifles.

But there is another school of thought that takes the prophet absolutely literally. Somehow this warfare will revert to old-fashioned weapons. We have already seen that the use of horses, though regarded as quite archaic, might be uniquely practical in this particular conflict.

A suggestion has been made many times relating to the oil shortage in the world, and how it might stop all machines someday. Man might revert to more primitive means if his machines fail, but he will never stop his warmaking. The soldier with a jammed rifle is glad to have a bayonet, and becomes a man with a spear.

This is most speculatory, but here and there are tempting hints of such things. The Russians have perfected an actual wooden rifle. They have compressed wood until it is harder than steel, but lighter to carry. It is still combustible. The Germans used some wooden bullets during World War II; they were cheaper to make and had pretty much the desired effect. In fact, they had the virtue of keeping the Allies' doctors overrun with surgery in the fields, since the bullets shattered in flesh and became infectious splinters.

Up-to-date news about poachers shooting bears (for meat!) in the American national parks tells of the use of crossbows instead of rifles. Quieter, cheaper, just as accurate, and just as deadly!

It is difficult to imagine a modern nation fielding a land army outfitted with the ancient weapons, however. But, again, it has proved equally difficult to disagree with a biblical prophet.

Another idea might be that the fire itself is unconventional. Ordinary fire burns wood, but nuclear fire burns metal. God's great fire from heaven that stops the invasion has been considered as a reference to thermonuclear phenomenon. Perhaps the Israelis will have the means to actually burn modern armored weaponry.

Still another speculation on this seven-year fire is acetylene, used in torches that cut, rather than burn, metal. It is still fire, and we do use it to destroy metal, such as in train-wreck rescues.

All these exercises, again, are mere speculation to try to uncover the meanings of Ezekiel's prophecies. But they serve the good purpose of demonstrating that prophecy is not to be summarily discarded because of its archaic language or ancient-seeming settings. Men have learned slowly but surely not to scoff at even the most "dated" terminology of Bible references. As the oft-quoted Ecclesiastes 1:9 puts it, "There is no new thing under the sun."

With the beginning of the seven-year fire, the Russo-Israeli war concludes. There is certainly no doubt of the victor. The aftermath of the war apparently exceeds all post-conflict carnages in man's long history of war. The scavenger beasts and birds are only cheated of their foul prey by full-time burial squads, with the participation of "all the people of the land" and travelers besides. Seven months to bury the dead, seven years to consume the residue of armaments in fire.

What was it all for? For the greater glory of God. Specifically, to testify of the power and the compassion of the Lord, and to explain at last the four-thousand-year tragedy of the chosen people.

For the benefit of the Gentiles, God has shown His glory:

> And I will set my glory among the heathen, and all the heathen shall see my judgment that I have executed, and my hand that I have laid upon them (Ezekiel 39:21).

For the benefit of the Jews, God has staged this miraculous victory:

> So the house of Israel shall know that I am the LORD their God from that day and forward (v. 22).

And for the benefit of all, the lesson Ezekiel tried to teach is repeated:

> The house of Israel went into captivity for their iniquity: because they trespassed against me, therefore hid I my face from them, and gave them into the hand of their enemies: so fell they all by the sword (v. 23).

Indeed, all of the prophecies portrayed by Ezekiel's painful demonstrations—the mortification of the prophet before the people's eyes—came to pass just as God originally said they would:

> According to their uncleanness and according to their transgressions have I done unto them, and hid my face from them (v. 24).

Chapter 39, the conclusion of this great prophecy which began with the dry bones vision and culminated in the

Russo-Israeli war, has a happy ending for the Jews. They are to be reconciled to God:

> When I have brought them again from the people, and gathered them out of the enemies' lands, and am sanctified in them in the sight of many nations; Then shall they know that I am the LORD their God, which caused them to be led into captivity among the heathen: but I have gathered them into their own land, and have left none of them any more there (vv. 27-28).

The section ends with a wonderful promise by God that He will not chastise Israel again and that He has now made the ultimate effort to secure His people:

> Neither will I hide my face any more from them: for I have poured out my spirit upon the house of Israel, saith the Lord God (v. 29).

This final blessing has the characteristic of a Messianic deliverance and has caused many interpreters to feel that the battle described earlier is actually the battle of Armageddon. Armageddon immediately precedes the advent of the millennial kingdom, which at last brings real peace.

This is a possible case, but we feel that there are enough distinguishing characteristics between the Russian invasion and the war called Armageddon to consider them to be separate conflicts. We think, however, that the results of the Russian invasion lead directly to Armageddon.

In the next chapter we will discuss this war to truly end all wars. No discussion of the affairs of mankind would be complete without Armageddon, the net result of man's efforts without God.

Apparently the demonstration of disaster that is the Russian invasion of Israel is insufficient to impress the world to seek salvation with God. "All the heathen shall see my judgment that I have executed" (v. 21), says the Lord, but somehow all the heathen get embroiled in Armageddon.

Men will see God in action but will still reject Him. There is no new thing under the sun.

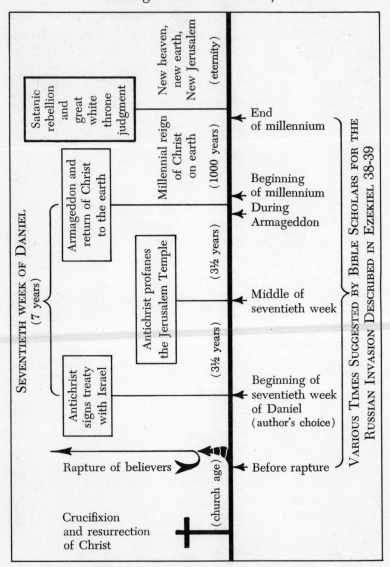

5

Satan on the Battlefield:
The Armageddon

THE RUSSIAN INVASION of Israel, in all its horror and devastation, will be only a curtain raiser.

Men will achieve much more in the Armageddon. In this chapter we're going to talk about *war!*

This global catastrophe will involve the entire race of man. No nation will escape. It is within reason to expect a billion casualties. Jesus said that if He were to delay His return, during this conflict "there would be no flesh saved" (Mt 24:22).

Our two world wars, and all that went before and since among the races and nations of mankind, will be regarded as so much petty quibbling compared to this grand finale. All of man's most sophisticated science and technology will be placed in the service of his most primal lusts. Power-maddened armies numbering in the hundreds of millions will fall upon the holy land and upon each other, and only the patient God of our creation will be able to still the tide.

The Armageddon conflict grows out of the Russian invasion of Israel. There is a great deal of uncertainty on this particular prophetic point. That the Russian invasion will happen is clear, but just when, and how it is juxtaposed with the other issues of the End Times, has raised some controversy.

The problem is the placement of the invasion itself. It precedes Armageddon, but it is not completely clear how *far* before it. Some hold it to be a part of Armageddon, and some have it very much before the great war. The accompanying chart shows that scholars have attempted to place the grisly work of Gog and Magog at almost every point along the future prophetic timetable.

The problem of comparing different prophets and scheduling, as it were, their different foreseen events on a future timetable has its hazards. There are very good arguments for each of the positions shown on the chart.

It is our conviction that the Russian invasion of Israel will take place at a point very close to the beginning of the tribulation period—Daniel's seventieth week. This is the moment when the Antichrist comes forward with his solution to the tensions in the Middle East and his infamous covenant with Israel (Daniel 9:27).

Daniel's seventieth week is calculated to last seven years, during which the great End-Time prophecies will run their course until the second coming of Christ to the earth. The indication by Ezekiel (Daniel's contemporary) that Israel will spend seven years gathering up the debris from the Russian invasion to use for fuel, is a tempting corollary to the seventieth week.

Could Daniel's seventieth week and Ezekiel's seven years refer to the same time period? We think this is highly plausible, and this is one of the reasons why we suggest that the Russian invasion of Israel will occur somewhere near the beginning point of the tribulation period.[1]

1. For a complete analysis of the prophecy of the tribulation period and the actions of the Antichrist in connection with it, see Thomas McCall and Zola Levitt, *Satan in the Sanctuary* (Chicago: Moody, 1973).

Possibly the annihilation of Russia as a military force will set the stage for the Antichrist's rise to power. He represents the revived Roman Empire, the ten-nation confederacy of Europe, and thus he would profit by the removal of this major rival for world domination. Israel would also be ripe for some peacemaker after the experience of the Russian invasion, even in victory.

Armageddon will come about through mismanagement by the Antichrist. He will first deliver on his promise to Israel; peace will prevail in the holy land for half of the tribulation period—three and one-half years. During this time the Antichrist will set up an effective world domination, steadily gaining economic and political control over the nations. Everyone will buy and sell everything in accordance with the fiscal system of the Antichrist (Rev 13: 17), and even the very elect of God—the Jews—will be fooled by the calm before the storm.

Only in these days of computers and numerical designations like credit card numbers and social security can we fully appreciate a world financial system. It used to take some imagination to see how in the world the Antichrist could ever pull this off, but in these days of common currency and common markets it will seem quite natural. In fact, it will seem like a great improvement over the past.

And perhaps it will be, in some ways, but the Antichrist will not be able to control his lust for power. When his total socio-politico-economic system is functioning on a worldwide scale, he will decide that he needs a title.

He will proclaim himself God!

It takes a special kind of egomaniac to choose that highest of titles. The Antichrist will not mean that he is *like*

God, or has the virtual *power* of God over men; he will declare that he *is* God!

In 2 Thessalonians 2:4 the apostle Paul pictures that one-of-a kind blasphemy. "He as God sitteth in the temple of God, showing himself that he is God."

The Antichrist will enter the Tribulation Temple, the third Jerusalem Temple, which will stand at this time, and plainly announce that he is God. Jesus specified that this "abomination of desolation," foreseen earlier by the prophet Daniel, would happen "in the holy place" of the Temple—the sacred sanctuary where God was said to dwell among His people (Matthew 24:15).

This incredible act clearly identifies the power behind the Antichrist. It is Satan's desire to replace God on earth; the Scriptures testify to this ongoing conflict since Satan's fall from heaven. The Antichrist will be Satan's most successful attempt to replace the Almighty. In the manner that God sent His Son to the earth, Satan will send the Antichrist, another resurrected "savior."

But it won't "jive in Jerusalem." The Jews have always regarded blasphemy as the highest of crimes, and they will recoil in horror from this action by their former mentor.

When Jesus identified Himself as the Son of God, there was much controversy among the Jews. The gospels tell of scenes of argument and whispered speculation about the remarkable Teacher of Galilee. The nation officially did not accept their Messiah, though enough Jews did that a church of Jerusalem was founded and the Word was promulgated to the world.

But this time—the Antichrist's time—there will be no such controversy. Israel will revolt.

From that moment on, the Antichrist's uneasy world

peace will be shattered. The blasphemy occurs at the mid-point of the seven-year tribulation period, so that three and one-half years are left to the mobilizations, invasions, and conflicts of the world armies leading up to the ultimate battle of Armageddon. The collision course is set when the Antichrist enters the temple and proclaims himself God. He will become Satan on the battlefield.

Daniel chronicles an attack by kings of the north and south against the Antichrist in Israel. Apparently, once the fragile peace is ruined, men will at once resort to their former ways. Israel's revolt will show the Antichrist to be less than supernatural, and may inspire widespread revolution against the dictator. Perhaps the attacking powers will consider the Antichrist's hold on things to be weakened by the Israeli revolt.

In any case, "The king of the south [will] push at him: and the king of the north shall come against him like a whirlwind," says Daniel (11:40). The Antichrist will have his hands full.

Many competent interpreters of prophecy have equated this king of the north with Ezekiel's Gog, who perpetrated the Russian invasion. This is one of the controversies existing about just when the Russian invasion occurs in the scheme of things. Naturally, if the king of the north is Gog, then the Russian invasion would occur after the Antichrist's blasphemy, or after the halfway point of the tribulation period. The king of the north reacts to Israel's revolt.

But we are disinclined to equate these two invaders. Ezekiel's Gog comes from the "uttermost north," and Daniel's king of the north is discussed in connection with his prophecies about the Greco-Syrian powers. We have already seen that Russia fits best the description of Gog's land for many reasons. In considering the king of the north, we must take into account Daniel's context. Daniel discusses, in chronological order, the four powers of Bible history, and his king of the north comes up in connection with the third such power—the Greco-Syrian power. The section Daniel 11:40-45 describes a purely Middle Eastern conflict, closer to home than the allied powers that descend in the invasion of Ezekiel 38 and 39.

Thus we are persuaded that the Russian invasion is separate from, and previous to, the invasion of the king of the north. As we understand the scenario, it will be Syria, united with Egyptian powers (the king of the south) who will attack the Antichrist and Israel.

Again, we do not sound very revolutionary to suggest that someday Egypt and Syria will mount a simultaneous attack against Israel. This is happening at the time of this writing.

But let's give credit where it's due. Daniel said it twenty-six centuries ago!

The present Middle Eastern conflicts are not to be confused with these future prophetic events, of course, but we can certainly see the stage being set. What an advantage we have over commentators of the past who could not even see an Israeli nation (before 1948), let alone these alliances and invasions. If we live long enough, we will see all prophecy fulfilled.

This invasion by the kings of the north and south ignites the whole of the world. The Antichrist will call upon his western forces, the ten-nation confederacy of Europe, and the kings of the east (probably indicating the massive hordes of China) will join in.

That will be a dramatic moment! From what we can gather, a 200,000,000-man army will *march* to the scene of the conflict in Israel from the east! (Revelation 9:16).

The mighty Euphrates River, which would present quite an obstacle to a marching army from the east, will be dried up in the end times, according to prophecy. The Asian horde, fully as large as the entire population of the United States today, will wreak real havoc on this terrible venture. They will account for the wiping out of a third of the earth's population (Revelation 9:18).

It all becomes very reasonable, if terrifying. Two hundred million soldiers was an unthinkable number at the time John wrote his astonishing book of Revelation, but we can see today that China would be able to field such an army. And uniquely, while China is the only power who could assemble such numbers, she is not equipped to transport them by mechanized means. If China seriously wanted to invade the Middle East, she would indeed be obliged to *walk* there! She does not have the ships and planes for transporting any sort of large army, let alone the behemoth foreseen by John.

So these are the combatants: the kings of the east, north, and south, and the European confederacy of the Antichrist. Israel will be stage-center as usual; she won't have to travel anywhere to participate in this war.

Russia has already been neutralized by the stunning catastrophe of the earlier invasion of Israel. As for the other nations, the world is too small to escape the holocaust. The United States, not specifically mentioned in prophecy, will likely either be allied with the European confederacy (such as now in NATO) or be a helpless casualty of global thermonuclear effects. These are suggested by repeated descriptions of raining fire, brimstone, smoke, and so on found in connection with these final conflicts.

THE BATTLE OF ARMAGEDDON

It's not quite clear who fights with whom about what. Getting there, as we have seen, is half the war.

Armageddon is a different kind of war than we have experienced in the history of our wars, not just in its scope but in its quality of supernatural events. Utilizing the same source—the Bible—which gives all the events leading up to this battle (and all of the fulfilled prophecy of the past), we find a curious story replete with divine actions.

Zechariah covers the action of the war and gives in ominous tones the perennial hazards of making war on Jerusalem and Israel: "Behold, I will make Jerusalem a cup of trembling unto all the people round about, when they shall be in the siege both against Judah and against Jerusalem. And in that day will I make Jerusalem a burdensome stone for all people: all that burden themselves with it shall be cut in pieces, though all the people of the earth be gathered against it" (12:2-3).

All those who tangle with Jerusalem will be "cut in pieces" indeed, and then some! Despite the best efforts of the world's most capable and fanatic invaders through four thousand years of bloody conflict, Jerusalem has survived, and it will continue to survive.

The huge world forces come together where they have room to do their fearsome work—in the valley of Megiddo in quiet Galilee. In that valley, "called in the Hebrew tongue Armageddon" (Rev. 16:16), untold millions of soldiers armed with the ultimate weapons of war will stage mankind's most effective attempt at suicide. Blood will flow, according to Revelation, "up to the bridles of the horses" (14:20).

Jerusalem, nearly one hundred miles away from the combat zone, will not be spared the effects of this horrifying conflict. Zechariah laments, "The city shall be taken, and the houses rifled, and the women ravished; and half of the city shall go forth into captivity" (14:2). Considering the pure numbers of the invading forces, no portion of little Israel will be safe from actual combat. And Jerusalem, God's city, veteran of invasions, rapings, and lootings from time immemorial, will have to endure this one last catastrophe.

But in this final hour of terrible conflict, something miraculous will transpire among the people of Israel. Pressed to the wall, their promised land torn apart in vicious war, their historic fears of national annihilation coming to reality before their eyes, the Jews turn to God. They have always done this, but in this case they turn to their Messiah— at last! It seems that the testimony of the 144,000 Hebrew Christians, who minister on earth after the rapture and who share the faith in Christ, at last gets a hearing in Israel.

Jesus said clearly enough, "No one comes to the Father, but through me" (John 14:6), and the Jews, in a time when their need to come to the Father is greater than ever before, will turn to their native Son, the carpenter of Nazareth. Jesus will be accepted as the true Messiah of Israel.

Isaiah 53, the conscience of the Jewish people, will be read with new understanding in Israel. "He is despised and rejected. . . . We esteemed him not. We hid . . . our faces from him. . . . But He was wounded for our transgressions,

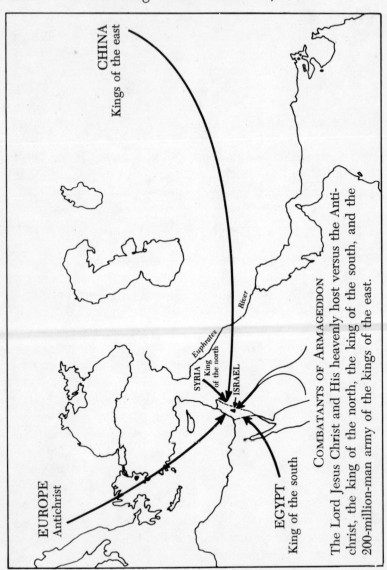

COMBATANTS OF ARMAGEDDON

The Lord Jesus Christ and His heavenly host versus the Antichrist, the king of the north, the king of the south, and the 200-million-man army of the kings of the east.

he was bruised for our iniquities" (vv 3, 5). Whether out of the desperation of the tragic moment, or from the testimony of the Christian witnesses, or from a national realization that disaster has ever followed the Jews since the time of Christ, the Jewish nation will completely awake to Christ. They will finally say, "Blessed is He who comes in the name of the Lord."

This is the password to salvation for the Jews. Jesus told them, while He was on the subject of the destruction of Jerusalem in His prophecy (Matthew 23:37-39) that He would not return until they welcomed Him in the words of Psalm 118:26: "Blessed is He that cometh in the name of the LORD."

It will be the greatest spiritual awakening in all of history, as the Jews come to Christ by the millions. It will be a true Day of Atonement in Israel: "In that day there shall be a fountain opened to the house of David and to the inhabitants of Jerusalem for sin and uncleanness (Zechariah 13:1) "And so all Israel will be saved" (Romans 11:26).

God is practical. He promised deliverance to Israel when the nation was faithful. He demonstrated this in bringing His chosen out of Egypt in a miraculous deliverance in the time of Moses. He will do no less in the time of the Armageddon.

The Jews receive Christ in a moment, as it were. There is no time to build a lot of churches or to ponder a lot of Scripture when Armageddon is going on in your land. The nation is saved, as a nation, instantaneously and on the battlefield. It is as if an electric current of truth is shot through everyone at once.

God's rewards are immediate.

The tide of Armageddon changes abruptly as the Lord imbues Israel with newfound military strength. The weakest buck private in the field will fight like King David, and the generals will be like God in battle: "In that day shall the LORD defend the inhabitants of Jerusalem; and he that is feeble among them at that day shall be as David; and the house of David shall be as God. . . . And it shall come to pass in that day, that I will seek to destroy all the nations that come against Jerusalem" (Zechariah 12:8-9).

The Israelis have been tough before, in the Six-Day War and the Yom Kippur War, but the world hasn't seen anything yet. The Lord Himself will come to lead His people in this final world war. "Then shall the LORD go forth, and fight against those nations, as when he fought in the day of battle. And his feet shall stand in that day upon the Mount of Olives" (Zechariah 14:3-4).

Jesus will return to His beloved Mount of Olives, adjacent to the Jerusalem Temple site, where He used to retire in the evenings for His own prayers. And cataclysmic things will happen. Militarily, those who attacked Jerusalem are in for a bad time of it, to say the least. "The LORD will smite all the people that have fought against Jerusalem; Their flesh shall consume away while they stand upon their feet, and their eyes shall consume away in their holes, and their tongue shall consume away in their mouth" (Zechariah 14:12).

John's Revelation sees a magnificent scene of Jesus arriving on a white horse at the head of a heavenly army: "And I saw heaven opened, and behold a white horse; and he that sat upon him was called Faithful and True, and in righteousness he doth judge and make war. . . . And the armies which were in heaven followed him upon white horses, clothed in fine linen, white and clean" (19:11, 14).

Revelation 19 goes on to picture fowls eating the flesh of kings, captains, and mighty men. The Antichrist "and the kings of the earth, and their armies" (v. 19) attempt war with Christ and His heavenly troops, with predictable outcome. John sees no scenes of lengthy battle, and Revelation goes immediately to the disposal of the Antichrist and his schemes for world domination. He gets the "lake of fire" (v. 20).

The troops of the Antichrist, who represent of course the enormous armies of the Gentile nations of the world, are "slain with the sword of him that sat upon the horse . . . and all the fowls were filled with their flesh" (v. 21).

This supernatural ending to the battle of Armageddon is not new in biblical accounts. We may say that there are natural wars and supernatural wars in connection with Jewish history, which is the story of a people whose destiny is controlled by God. The deliverance of the Jews from Egypt showed the loss of the Egyptian forces when they tried to cross the Red Sea on the dry land used by the Jews.

David experienced a supernatural victory over Goliath in response to his faithfulness. Joshua demolished the walls of Jericho with trumpets. The Maccabees experienced the miraculous touch of God when they defeated Antiochus and rededicated the second Temple.

Armageddon follows suit, demonstrating that God responds to true faith. When the Gentile nations first march against the holy land, they certainly have no fear of the little Israeli army. They plunder Jerusalem and set up their bloodletting in Galilee, indifferent to the great people whose land they desecrate.

But what a different story when the Jews turn to Christ! How shocking for the Gentiles to suddenly face an army of King Davids with Jesus Christ at the head of it!

We have not experienced a supernatural war for some time. The Russian invasion of Israel, with its strange annihilation of the invading forces, is the first of this final period. On that occasion the issue is atheism versus faith in God, and as we have seen, God takes a hand in it. It is almost a smaller picture of the vicious Armageddon to follow.

Armageddon, thankfully, is the end of every kind of war. It marks the return of Jesus to the earth for an extended stay and a new kingdom. The great age of "peace on earth, good will toward men" is ushered in at the climax of Armageddon.

With this period of world cataclysm, begun with the Russian invasion of Israel and ended with the Armageddon, out of the way, let's look to happier times. Our discussion would not be complete without an encouraging look at the return of Jesus Christ.

6

"Thy Kingdom Come"

JESUS WILL NOT RETURN strictly for His military mission. We can be thankful enough that the battle at Armageddon is stopped short of annihilating all mankind, but the Lord will return for a greater purpose. He will establish the first successful, peaceful, equitable world government. His will shall be "done in earth, as it is in heaven."

The inexorable series of cataclysmic events proceeding from the Russian invasion of Israel goes on, as Jesus occupies His throne of glory and confronts what is left of man's broken-down world.

How Did You Treat My Brothers?

First Jesus will judge the nations of the world—the Gentiles.

This will be quite a different Jesus from the sacrificial lamb of the gospels. The Saviour, who endured humiliation, torture, and physical death at the hands of the unbelieving, will return as a Lion.

He had taught His followers to pray, "Thy kingdom come, Thy will be done, in earth as it is in heaven" (Matthew 6:9), and He will see to it that this prayer is answered at once.

Here is how things will stand as the Lord operates His

immigration office into the new kingdom: the Gentiles of the world, the survivors of Armageddon, will be judged; for two other groups the judgment process will be waived. One of these will be the unique group of past believers— those of Old Testament times and of the church age, along with those believers who died as martyrs in the Tribulation. They will be resplendent in their resurrection bodies. The remaining group will be the Christian nation of Israel.

As we have seen, all Israel will be redeemed at what looked to be its final hour. They will have carte blanche into the millennial kingdom, as will all other believers. As Paul exulted, "All Israel shall be saved" (Romans 11:26).

And that takes care of everybody. The dividing line is Christ, who says, "If you are not *for* Me, you are *against* Me."

Israel will take its guaranteed place as "the head [of the nations] and not the tail" (see Deuteronomy 28:13). Jesus will judge and govern in Jerusalem, the new world capital in the Millennium. All the law of the world will emanate from Jerusalem as, in a way, it always did.

Now back to the Gentiles who will stand trial before Jesus. They will at least have a fair Judge, but the issue of whether they have believed or not will have really caught up with them this time.

Jesus will ask, "How did you treat My brothers?" The beautiful chapter, Matthew 25, gives a transcript of that future courtroom scene:

> When the Son of man shall come in his glory, and all the holy angels with him, then shall he sit upon the throne of his glory: And before him shall be gathered all nations: and he shall separate them one from another, as a shepherd divideth his sheep from the goats; and he shall set

the sheep on his right hand, but the goats on the left (vv. 31-33).

Nobody gets to testify because, by the Lord's criteria, they already have. After He separates the defendants into the two groups, He will explain,

> Then shall the King say unto them on his right hand, Come, ye blessed of my Father, inherit the Kingdom prepared for you from the foundation of the world:

> For I was an hungred, and ye gave me meat: I was thirsty, and ye gave me drink: I was a stranger and ye took me in: Naked, and ye clothed me: I was sick, and ye visited me: I was in prison, and ye came unto me (vv. 34-36).

These defendants, the sheep, are incredulous. They have never seen Jesus. They are honest enough to say so:

> Lord, when saw we thee an hungred, and fed thee? or thirsty, and gave thee drink? (v. 37).

And they cover all the categories given above by the Lord. They are not aware that they have greatly honored the Lord by their right doings in the tribulation period.

Jesus explains to them:

> Verily I say unto you, Inasmuch as ye have done it unto one of the least of these my brethren, ye have done it unto me (v. 40).

Happily, the sheep receive full credit for their faith and acts of love during the difficult time of the Antichrist.

Jesus' brethren are the Jews, particularly the 144,000 Jews who suffered the tribulation period in unflinching faith in the Lord and stalwart witnessing to the lost. In a larger sense, all mankind are Jesus' brethren since He became a man on our behalf. But the context here dictates the "brethren" in question as the Lord's fellow Jews.

Had the sheep been Bible students, they would not have been at all surprised at their acquittal in Jesus' courtroom. God said plainly in Genesis 12:3, the stirring moment of the Abrahamic covenant, "I will bless them that bless thee" (the Jewish nation). As we have seen, God's covenant with His Chosen People is to endure to eternity, as it always has. Jesus would not be expected to condemn those who blessed the Jews.

But God went on to tell Abraham in that same Scripture, "I will curse them that curse thee," and we now come to the goats, the defendants on Jesus' left.

They failed to exercise benevolence to those in need in the hard times. "For I was an hungred, and ye gave me no meat: I was thirsty, and ye gave me no drink" (Matthew 25:42). They too question their Judge, on the same basis as the sheep brought up. "When did we fail? When did we even *see* You?"

The Lord applies the same precedent:

> Verily I say unto you, Inasmuch as ye did it not to one of the least of these, ye did it not to me (v. 45).

They couldn't ask for a fairer trial.

Their sentence is a tough one. They fare no better than the devil and his henchmen. "Depart from me," pronounces the Lord, "into everlasting fire, prepared for the devil and his angels" (v. 41).

Admission to the millennial kingdom for Gentiles, then, rests on whether they demonstrated faith in Christ by showing kindness to the suffering chosen people in their final hour. There will be some Gentiles, then, who will go through the Tribulation, believe in Christ, and have their hearts in the right place toward the suffering; and so they will obtain a place in the kingdom. They will not become rulers, as age-of-grace Christians will, but they will become subjects in that glorious and peaceful world by just showing a little kindness.

It seems like an ultimately fair criterion. Is there really a person alive who cannot see the good of feeding the hungry, comforting the sick, and clothing the naked? Can Jesus' principles have been so covered over by a relentlessly wicked world that no one will respond in sympathy?

Not hardly! The principle of salvation by faith is not relaxed at this remarkable litigation, but an individual might be spared for the smallest show of human mercy. And we all have the potential for mercy. We still are, after all, created in the image of God.

It won't be easy to assist the enemies of the Antichrist in such times. Obviously the punishment will be severe on earth for those who have anything to do with God or His Chosen People. The Antichrist is "god" during the tribulation, as he duly proclaims, and any valid worship of the true God or of His principles would be a kind of inverse blasphemy.

On the other hand, opportunities to do the right thing will abound. The vocal 144,000 Hebrew Christian preachers will be a helpless target of the atheistic forces at large in the world. They will likely be jailed, hungry, and otherwise abused. They will certainly need the kind of help the Lord specified for His brethren. At risk of death, courageous believers will still qualify, according to the Scripture.

And that is how this first judgment day will proceed. Basically we have just two groups—believers, with a free pass into the kingdom, and unbelievers who will flunk the entrance exam.

Where do *you* stand?

KING OF KINGS

Once the membership of the new kingdom is settled, it gets immediately underway.

Kingdoms on earth never really have worked out very well. Typically, the monarch connived and cheated behind the scenes while the people sang, "God save the king." But it's a completely different story when God *is* the King!

The sinless, compassionate, incorruptible King will make all the difference in the millennium, despite the fact that to some degree, men will still be up to their old tricks. Isaiah gives us an unforgettable picture of the power and abilities of Jesus as King:

> For unto us a child is born, unto us a son is given: and the government shall be upon his shoulder: and his name shall be called Wonderful, Counsellor, The mighty God, The everlasting Father, The Prince of Peace.
>
> Of the increase of his government and peace there shall be no end, upon the throne of David, and upon his kingdom, to order it, and to establish it with judgment and with justice from henceforth even for ever. The zeal of the LORD of hosts will perform this (9:6-7).

What was not entirely clear to the Jews who read their Scriptures was the two-phase appearance of Jesus on earth. The essence of Christianity—that there was to be first an appearance characterized by the Messiah's rejection and suffering—was overlooked, although it is prophesied clearly (and by the same prophet):

He is despised and rejected of men; a man of sorrows, and acquainted with grief. . . . Surely he hath borne our griefs, and carried our sorrows. . . . But he was wounded for our transgressions, he was bruised for our iniquities: the chastisement of our peace was upon him; and with his stripes we are healed. All we like sheep have gone astray; we have turned every one to his own way; and the Lord hath laid on him the iniquity of us all (53:3-6).

Somehow, though the kingship of the Messiah was certainly realized by the Jews—they *still* expect their kingly Messiah—His sacrifice aspect was missed, despite this passage and many like it in the Old Testament. Alternate interpretations for these revelations are given by Jewish scholars. But as we have seen, the chosen people are to come to the full realization of their Messiah's mission and will welcome Him as King. Their promised land is to become truly the center of the earth.

The necessity of the delay between the Lord's two comings was lost on the Jews, since their Old Testament theology did not reveal a period like the church age. During this period, Christ reached the world with His gospel. The Jews, already the Chosen People, have never felt that they needed this special provision.

The Church, as the body of believers reached during the interim period is called, is to marry Jesus before He assumes His earthly throne. John pictures this great wedding in heaven and refers to the Church as the Bride of Christ. (Revelation 19:7).

Following that, Jesus returns with His bride to the earth and occupies His throne of David.

The Christians, then, are originally raptured, or "caught up" to heaven to be with Jesus through the hard times of the tribulation period on earth, and then they are wed to the Lord. Finally they return with Him and enjoy their promised privileges of ruling in the millennial kingdom. The population of the kingdom is completed when the Christians return with the Lord to join those on the earth who have qualified for the kingdom by their faith in Christ and their good works toward the Lord's brethren in the tribulation. The latter completely qualify as true believers.

Thus peopled purely with believers, the kingdom will do well and survive a long time. John reveals in Revelation 20 that the kingdom will endure a thousand years, and hence it is called the millennium (*mille*-thousand; *annum*-year).

Peace on Earth

As King, Jesus achieves what no other ruler has accomplished—peace. For one thousand years the world will experience no war at all.

The Antichrist, with his supernatural powers and huge armies, maintains world peace for a brief period between the Russian invasion of Israel and the Armageddon, but it is the cold war peace we are all familiar with.

Jesus brings the peace foreseen by Isaiah:

> And they shall beat their swords into plowshares, and their spears into pruninghooks: nation shall not lift up sword against nation, neither shall they learn war anymore (2:4).

The United Nations building in New York City bears a portion of this worthy Scripture on its entrance, but unfortunately it is quoted without the full context. Missing is the first statement of Isaiah 2:4, "And He shall judge among the nations." God has been left out, as usual. It is

"THY KINGDOM COME . . . IN EARTH, AS IT IS IN HEAVEN"

not until the Lord makes His judgments among the nations that the kingdom and its full-time peace will prevail.

How ironic for the world's most celebrated peace-makers to quote from a Book which contains the solutions to all of their problems, but fail to read the whole book, or even the whole Scripture that they find suitable.

This world has at least a five-thousand-year history of war with no indications that it will ever be otherwise. Even today, modern man, conqueror of so much disease, tamer of nature, explorer of space, still spends most of his time and money fighting. "Defense" claims the riches of every modern nation in proportion to its size, and man's ultimate scientific know-how goes into killing (or, a new term adjusted to our times, overkilling).

The Bible analyzes the problem as a basic maladjustment of men to their Creator, and thus to one another. Jesus said, "Peace I give unto you" (John 14:27), and those in relationship to Him know the deepest meaning of this promise. But it will take His very reappearance to accomplish this over the whole of the earth, and then only when the unbelievers have almost killed out their kind. Sad.

But Isaiah's fondest visions of peace will be achieved when the Lord returns. Isaiah sees enthusiastic, spiritually motivated people of the world going up to Jerusalem in the millennium and taking a real interest in government:

> And it shall come to pass in the last days that the mountain of the LORD's house shall be established in the top of the mountains [at the Jerusalem temple site[1]] and shall be exalted above the hills; and all nations shall flow unto

1. See Thomas McCall and Zola Levitt, *Satan in the Sanctuary*, pp. 108-10.

it. And many people shall go and say, Come ye, and let us go up to the mountain of the LORD, to the house of the God of Jacob; and He will teach us of his ways, and we will walk in His paths: for out of Zion [Israel] shall go forth the law, and the word of the LORD from Jerusalem (2:2-3).

Worthy subjects of a worthy king! Those will be the days!

This remarkable change in world affairs will affect even the animals. They will all become peace lovers. Isaiah says,

The wolf also shall dwell with the lamb, and the leopard shall lie down with the kid; and the calf and the young lion and the fatling together; and a little child shall lead them. . . . The lion shall eat straw like the ox (11:6-7).

The animals will live together and eat from the fields instead of killing each other as man has done. Even a little child need have no fear of wild animals in the peaceful times to come.

It will be a changed world in more ways than that. No one will die in the millennium, but children will be born. At first the population will be a little smaller than we are used to, but it will include, along with those we have specified, all the faithful Christians of the church age and the saved Old Testament believers. They will all be resurrected, like their King, and outfitted for immortality.

World history will be a strange subject, if it is discussed at all. It will be exceedingly difficult to convince the children that come along in the happy millennium that men once hated and killed one another. But the information will be available—particularly in the Bible, which, as we have seen, will be a steady topic of discussion in government circles. The Bible chronicles a lot of man's old ways of doing things, and Jesus observed that heaven and earth would pass away before this best-seller would go out of print. "The earth shall be full of the knowledge of the LORD, as the waters cover the sea," says Isaiah (11:9).

The twelve apostles will rule over the twelve tribes of Israel, as it enjoys true favored-nation status, and all of those who were "faithful in a very little" (Luke 19:17) will be given great responsibilities under the new regime.

No wonder the Lord urged His followers to pray, "Thy kingdom come!"

WATCH OUT, EGYPT!

The millennium sounds like a perfect world, but in some small ways it still is not. Amazingly enough, men will still insist on their rebellious ways, though to quite a lesser degree, even in that ultimate earthly utopia.

The fault lies deeply within the nature of men—in the sin nature they inherited from their common father, Adam. The men born during the millennium will have the same fatal flaw, and though they will maintain a peaceful world alongside the many believers, some tests of obedience will still be necessary.

Zechariah supplies that the Feast of Tabernacles, commemorating the deliverance of the Hebrew nation from slavery in Egypt to their promised land, will still be celebrated each year. And attendance will be mandatory!

> And it shall come to pass, that every one that is left of all the nations which came against Jerusalem shall even go up from year to year to worship the King, the LORD of hosts, and to keep the feast of tabernacles. And it shall be,

that whoso will not come up of all the families of the earth unto Jerusalem to worship the King, the LORD of hosts, even upon them shall be no rain (Zechariah 14:16-17).

And, as if the Lord knows full well just *who* among the family of nations might fail to appear for the grand old Jewish feast, He says,

And if the family of *Egypt* go not up, and come not, that [they will] have no rain; there shall be the plague, where with the LORD will smite the heathen that come not up to keep the feast of tabernacles (v. 18, italics added).

And yet again, as if a word to the wise were not going to be sufficient, He warns,

This shall be the punishment of *Egypt,* and the punishment of all nations that come not up to keep the feast of tabernacles (v. 19, italics added).

If Israel has ever had a dependable enemy it's Egypt, and somehow it appears than even in the millennium the Egyptians will be loath to offer this simple allegiance to the Lord. Perhaps the Scripture singles out Egypt for emphasis; that is, if Egypt is required to attend, then certainly all the other nations are, after all. We'll have to wait and see.

It makes a peculiar picture. There will be "heathen" in the millennium as it progresses. Men have always been free, and they will apparently continue to be free to choose God or not. But they *will* have to render this specified allegiance to Christ once each year. That's hardly as much allegiance as men now pay their respective unbelieving governments. But if they refuse even this small token, they will have some troubles. It's hard to plant when there's no rain. Particularly in places like Egypt.

As the centuries pass in the millennium, and as the population grows, a certain rebellious spirit seems to foment among the nations. Of course it does not come to war during the millennium, but at its very end there is something of a replay of the Russian invasion of Israel.

Satan has not been done away with, but has been bound helpless for the thousand-year period. At the end of the millennium he is released for one last try (in effect) at corrupting the world. And he finds armies available.

This final battle is given little space in the Scriptures. John's Revelation covers it in a few verses (20:7-10). Satan is defeated quickly, and this time banished to the eternal lake of fire, never to rise up again.

On to Eternity

We can't say much about eternity, because it is a totally supernatural phenomenon. At the end of the millennium, our story of the coming Russian invasion of Israel is finished; its steady chain of events is finally ended. The world will undergo a change unlike anything since creation.

God will revamp everything. There will be a new heaven, a new earth, and a new Jerusalem. There will be no more time. The oceans will disappear. John reports an incredible scene:

> "And I saw a new heaven and a new earth: for the first heaven and the first earth were passed away; and there was no more sea. And I John saw the holy city, new Jerusalem, coming down from God out of heaven, prepared as a bride adorned for her husband" (Revelation 21:1-2).

What kind of picture does that make? Where was John standing? What does a city coming down from the sky look like? Where did the first heaven and the first earth go?

Obviously, these are matters very much beyond the scope of today's observer. Perhaps those in the millennium, who have lived a thousand years and have seen Christ on the earth, will be able to confront such mysteries. There isn't space in this little book about war to discuss eternity.

Believers will be there, of course; but heaven only knows (literally!) what form we'll take. We can't live without water, and rain was needed even in the millennium, but in eternity there will be a new earth with no seas. We look up at the sky now and think of it as heaven, but that sky is going away somewhere, and a new one will be installed. What is under our foot the earth—will be something utterly new.

Another judgment will be held for entrance into eternity. This is the famed Judgment Day when Christ will open the book of life and will judge every unbelieving soul that ever walked this earth. The sea will give up her dead, and even hell will be opened to deliver up its dead (Revelation 20:12-13). The billions of souls who inhabited the eons of earthly time will be judged "according to their works," one by one!

"And whosoever was not found written in the book of life," concludes John, "was cast into the lake of fire" (20:15).

7

A Strategy for Christians

WHY IS GOD TELLING US all this?

Did prophecy ever save anybody? Will the fact that Christians quote the Bible about the future impress the unbelievers?

Perhaps, but cases in the Bible itself show otherwise. When Jeremiah shouted that the Babylonians were going to destroy Jerusalem and the mighty Temple of God, he was jailed for annoying the government. When Jesus, looking sadly at the great second Temple, said, "There shall not be left here one stone upon another" (Matthew 24:2), He was ridiculed by the unbelievers.

Yet, God chose to reveal His plans in advance to those who would read them. What is His purpose? What are we supposed to do?

This chapter is for Christians—those who believe in Jesus and His atoning work. The next chapter is for the unbelievers—practical suggestions for hard times ahead.

We put this one first because the Rapture might come before you finish this book.

We can suggest two reasons why God has chosen to reveal the future. One is timing. As we follow events as they happen, we get a very real sense of just where we are in God's scheme of things. The other reason is so we know the alternative to belief in Christ. That alternative is so horrible that it might well spur us to real efforts to reach this world for Christ.

This is a late hour for reaching the world, but remember the thief on the cross. He had but hours to live, but we'll see him in the kingdom!

Christians can relax, if we wish. The rapture will take us off this sinking ship and we'll be spared further grief. But in the good example of the One who laid down His very life for His friends, we can do better than that.

The apostle gave a word of advice for these times:

> And let us consider one another to provoke unto love and to good works: Not forsaking the assembling of ourselves together, as the manner of some is; but exhorting one another: and so much the more, as ye see the day approaching (Hebrews 10:24-25).

The "day approaching" is the Lord's day—the day when He'll commence judging. That day is the fulfillment of prophecy. "So much the more" should we heed this advice as that day approaches.

We are in a much better position than those at the time of the apostles to see the day approaching when it will be too late to help this world. We have our prophecy—our time schedule, as it were. We can check off events as they happen.

When we started to write this book, there was no Yom Kippur War as yet. There was no really reasonable thought of a Russian invasion of Israel in the offing. It would have shocked the world if Russia herself had invaded Israel at that time.

But a few months later, Russia did shock the world by reportedly mobilizing troops for that war!

We almost ticked off another event in just a few months. May God help us to get this prophecy book to you before it becomes a history book!

Back to the apostle's good advice. Believers are urged not to avoid gathering together and to exhort one another in our spiritual graces and good works. We are not to be spiritual hermits, exulting in the fact that our Lord is going to get us out of all this; we are rather to become actively involved with other believers in the wonderful thing that is faith in God.

The effect will be obvious. If believers can show the world a united, triumphant front in these troubled times, it may just cause some of the world to think. They may want to know why we are as we are, and we surely can tell them!

Our churches, our media, and all of our people—Christ's people—need to be stirred up to realize that our Lord gave us a great commission. We are to share the gospel; we are to preach "to every creature" (Mark 16:15).

When John had finished seeing his incredible revelation of the future, with all of the stupefying scenes of the last days of this whole creation, he began to witness. In his brief and beautiful way he said,

> And the Spirit and the bride say, Come. And let him that heareth say, Come. And let him who is thirsty come. And whosoever will, let him take the water of life freely (Revelation 22:17).

How fitting a statement: Let him take the water of life freely! In the millennium, the unbeliever who will not approach the Lord will have no rain. In eternity there is no sea. We have all the water that's left!

If knowing prophecy does not move us to share our faith, something is very wrong. To understand the condition and destiny of literally billions of unsaved people who are plunging headlong toward horrible lives and horrible deaths, to realize through prophecy that the very politics of today's world are rapidly bringing this to pass, to know in addition that a solution to all of this coming agony is readily available to all—to know all that is to be put in a position of the most solemn responsibility.

If we know all that and still fail to tell the world at every chance, then we are acting in an unchristian way.

HERE COMES THE BRIDE

The Bride of Christ, the Church, the body of believers, is this world's only chance. We must not fail in this. Our God is "not willing that any should perish" (2 Peter 3:9), and He commissioned us to do the hard work of reaching the lost. The Spirit and the Bride say, "Come."

When we say, "Come," we are extending quite an invitation. We are admitting our friends to the rapture, to the very wedding of Jesus Christ, to the millennial kingdom, and to everlasting life in eternity. And think what we are getting them *out* of!

When our friends accept our invitation to those coming spectacular events, they inherit all of our heaven-sent assurances immediately. And we who are believers today have the profoundly relieving assurance that we will not have to go through the tribulation period on earth. The rapture will come before that!

It is not entirely clear whether we will see the coming Russian invasion of Israel, however. We have placed it just at the beginning of the tribulation period—perhaps pre-

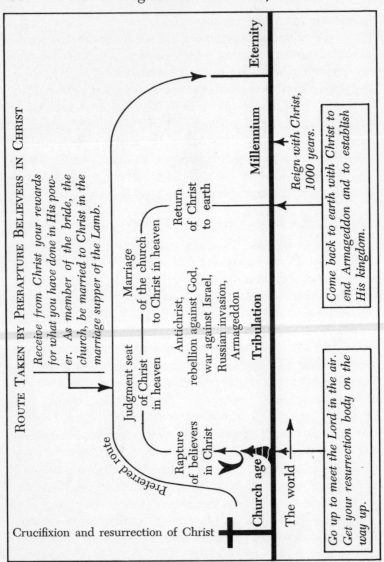

ROUTE TAKEN BY PRERAPTURE BELIEVERS IN CHRIST

Receive from Christ your rewards for what you have done in His power. As member of the bride, the church, be married to Christ in the marriage supper of the Lamb.

Crucifixion and resurrection of Christ

Church age

The world

Rapture of believers in Christ

Preferred route

Judgment seat of Christ in heaven

Marriage of the church to Christ in heaven

Antichrist, rebellion against God, war against Israel, Russian invasion, Armageddon

Return of Christ to earth

Tribulation

Millennium

Eternity

Go up to meet the Lord in the air. Get your resurrection body on the way up.

Come back to earth with Christ to end Armageddon and to establish His kingdom.

Reign with Christ, 1000 years.

ceding it slightly. We have cited that there are widely differing opinions on this, and that the rapture might occur at any moment. It is good to remember that nothing in prophecy has to happen before the rapture.

The events of Ezekiel 36 and 37 have happened before our eyes. We have seen the "dry bones"—the Jewish people scattered in the "graveyards" of the Gentile nations—regathered to the promised land. We have seen a nation form there and maintain itself for a quarter of a century. Ezekiel goes on with the Russian invasion of Israel immediately in his next chapters, 38 and 39, noting nothing to happen in between.

It is conjecture to assume that this means we will see the invasion, but we have the advantage over past analysts in that we live in times of real fulfillment of prophecy. From a purely worldly standpoint, it would surprise no one if Russia invaded Israel in the very near future.

The surprises would come in the results of that invasion.

Also, we might say that the point of the rapture is to spare the believers the real holocausts to come. The Russian invasion of Israel is a confined war, by the prophet's description. It would likely have little effect on the church, which is not found in great numbers in either Russia or the Middle East. The world has weathered the Yom Kippur War with its dreary outcome, and presumably could put up with that one, too, without undue damage.

Then again, there is the supernatural factor to consider. Logically, God would hold off the rapture as long as possible in order to gather as many souls to the harvest as He can. But He acts in a visible way in the Russian invasion. We have seen that fire comes down on the Russian armies, and unless this description relates to nuclear attack or something we can understand in an earthly way, God would be "exposing" Himself to the world.

It is held by many commentators that when God actually shows Himself by His actions, the age of faith is over.

In any case, we hold that the rapture and the Russian invasion of Israel are close together, near the beginning of the tribulation period. If we are right in that, signs of the Russian invasion are virtually signs of the rapture.

During that scary Yom Kippur week when the Russians reportedly were mobilizing troops, we seemed to be very close to fulfilling End-Times prophecy. That a situation very like that seen by Ezekiel could happen in these times certainly suggests that the fulfillment of his visions is quite possible, and maybe even very close.

As close as his chapter 38 is to his chapter 37!

So, in a way, we are rapidly becoming friends in need to our unbelieving fellow men. It's no longer a question of "Come to our church," but more like "Avoid the Antichrist and the Armageddon."

Our knowledge, which the Lord has imparted to us, is of inestimable value to the world. If we withhold it, we would be like researchers withholding a cure for cancer. We have the truth, and as our Lord said, "The truth shall make you free" (John 8:32).

We can calculate the timing of God's plan by watching our world. We can see the alternatives to going with God by just reading the prophecy in the Bible.

The strategy for Christians has been said before:

> And Jesus came and spake unto them, saying, All power is given unto me in heaven and in earth. Go ye therefore and teach all nations, baptizing them in the name of the

Father, and of the Son, and of the Holy Ghost: Teaching them to observe all things whatsoever I have commanded you: And, lo, I am with you alway, even unto the end of the world (Matthew 28:18-20).

8

A Strategy for Unbelievers

PERHAPS, DEAR READER, you do not believe in Christ and we have not persuaded you. Perhaps you have found this book to be good bedtime reading and an entertaining theory of things to come, but you figure you'll make out on your own wits as you always have.

Very well. First, please know that we love you.

We don't mean to sound fatuous, but we'd hardly be any sort of good representatives of Jesus Christ on earth if we failed to love all men as He commanded. But it is not just a matter of following His dictum. We are *able* to love you. Christianity has the peculiar effect of imbuing the plainest individuals with a real ability to love—even to love enemies, as our Lord also counseled. We do not regard you as an enemy, but more like a brother—a brother in great need.

So, if you will, we would like to make a few suggestions about the future. In view of all of the coming circumstances we have outlined, we think you should take action.

First of all, the Bible itself gives one imperative to unbelievers. "Believe on the Lord Jesus Christ, and thou shalt be saved" (Acts 16:31). We would be remiss to leave that out. We think it's still the only way to go.

Failing that, let's consider reasonable alternatives. Since the coming Russian invasion of Israel appears to be in preparation these days, and since that seems to start the whole chain of tragic events associated with the End Times, you'd better get moving!

Discussing the effects of the abortive Russian invasion, Ezekiel specifies that there will be fire on Magog and among those who dwell securely in the coastlands (see 39:6, NASB). This cryptic "coastlands" is more easily understood when we look at it in context with Ezekiel's world. In that Mediterranean area, most countries were more densely settled along their coasts to facilitate trade. Ships were the ultimate tool of international commerce. The present United States is still an example of more densely settled coastlands than inland areas. Ezekiel's term indicated the civilizations across the seas from Israel.

It is possible, then, that we Americans are counted among those "who dwell securely in the coastlands," and that this "fire" capable of wiping out the enormous allied forces of the Russian invasion will have its effects elsewhere. This is especially reasonable when we consider the overwhelming destruction of nuclear warfare and its resulting fallout.

Therefore, it would be good if you would now install a bombshelter capable of resisting atomic-scale warfare and radiation. People may think you're a bit paranoid, but they also laughed at Noah until it started to rain.

Fortunately, while the destruction resulting from the Russian invasion appears to be very widespread, it's over quickly, and the world goes on. Let us assume you have taken our advice about the bomb shelter and have survived. What next?

Next you should watch for the rapture of the church. This will be unmistakable. The Christians will plain disappear. Since they are to meet the Lord in the air, they will just be "gone" all at once. There's been a lot of conjecture about how this will happen and how it will be explained, but remember, we are dealing here with a period of divine activity, and lots of things are going to seem strange.

Conceivably, those two events—the invasion and the rapture—will be in the other order, as we have explained, but in any case, they'll be close together.

The one or the other may make a believer out of you. Jonah, who resisted the Lord's directives, had a real change of heart when he came back out of the great fish! But assuming that your faith in godlessness still persists, you are in for the long ride. Once the rapture has occurred, your chance to be airlifted out of all this is over. You can always still revert to Christ, but you'll have your troubles!

The next thing to watch for is the appearance of the Antichrist. This will occur right after the rapture, and, we think, right after the Russian invasion.

If you are a typical unbeliever of that day, you will say to the Antichrist, "Thank you. At last we're going to have peace"; and you will bow down to that glib egomaniac like all the others. You will note with distaste a continuing Christian activity, but you will be delighted to participate in the new regime of the tribulation period. You'll gladly have your number tattooed on your skin so that you can go shopping conveniently; and you'll think the world has at last pulled itself together.

Memories of this book and many others that warned about such things may come to your mind from time to time, but you'll think, "Those fellows had no appreciation for what men can accomplish when they get together."

The joke is on you!

You'll sigh with gladness over the peace in the Middle East, and you'll watch the Tribulation Temple, a truly magnificent piece of architecture, rise in Jerusalem. You will probably think, "You have to give those Jews credit. They really hang in there. When the going gets tough, the tough get going." (The Temple might be actually constructed ahead of these other events, but, in any case, it will be standing and functioning by the middle of the tribulation period.)

You'll watch with approval, if you are a typical unbeliever, as the Antichrist signs a treaty with Israel; and it will seem to you that the troublesome powder keg will at last be permanently defused.

But getting back to our suggestions for you, that treaty signing will start your last seven years, and you should act accordingly. It might be best to sell everything you have and get really far away from the Middle East. You're on your way to Armageddon.

You may chance across a witness for Christ at this late date. He may be one of those 144,000 preachers of Israel, and you may find him appealing for his very stubbornness and courage under fire.

May we recommend him to you? It still won't be too late. He'll provide you safe passage to the millennium if you'll believe.

But you may resist him because belief in Christ will be a very risky proposition at that point. The Antichrist will have everybody computerized, and the remaining Christians will be on the most stupendous "enemies list" of all

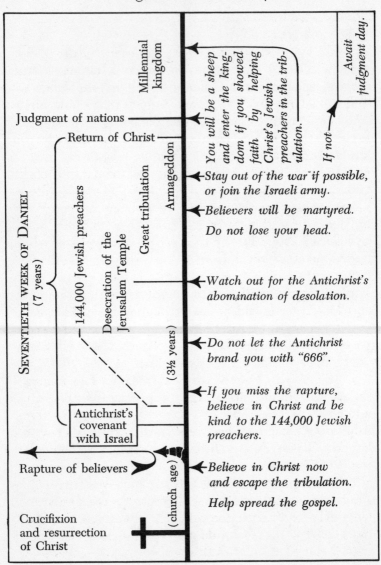

time. You may want to avoid that. You'll see Christians actually executed for their faith.

Frankly, we would encourage you to take this life-and-death risk. If you come to believe in the Lord Jesus, you will pass into the new kingdom. If you do not, sooner or later you will die forever. To resist out of fear would be to trade eternity for less than seven years of the worst possible earthly life. In this particular case, you are truly worth more dead than alive.

But at least be kind to that Hebrew Christian preacher. Remember, Jesus will take that behavior into consideration in the immigration office of the millennium. If you have the chance to feed a starving Jew, or to clothe him, or to comfort him while he is sick or in prison, for your own sake do so! Become a sheep and be separated from the goats!

Eventually you will see the Antichrist go into the new Jerusalem Temple and proclaim himself God. This may strike you as a bit egotistical, but we have tolerated such excesses in our leaders before. You'll probably go along with it.

At all costs, resist having the identifying number stamped on you if it has not been done already. You may go hungry for awhile because you will not be able to go through the checkout line at the local supermarket without your number, but you'll be better off foraging for food than being judged later on. It's not quite clear when that particular legislation will take place, but even under the Antichrist's computerized systems, it will take some time to number everybody in the world. You may have a chance to hold off. By all means, do so!

But if you go along with this too, your alternatives have

really run out. Assuming that you bear the Antichrist's number, have not taken the opportunity to be kind to the brethren of the Lord, and still do not believe in Jesus Christ, everything else will be done *for* you.

If you have never had the opportunity to visit Israel, you will go at government expense when you are drafted into the Antichrist's army. If you can, you should seek high ground in Israel because of virtual seas of blood as high as the bridles of the horses. If you can make yourself scarce enough to survive the demolishing of the Gentile forces by Jesus and His heavenly army, you will make it as far as the trial before the throne of Christ. But you will be a goat, and the verdict will be "everlasting punishment" (Mt 25:46).

We are not threatening you. We're just quoting the Book that contains all the rest of our information. We've seen too much of it come out to doubt it at this point.

We don't know precisely what that everlasting punishment will be, but we know about the alternative. Bear with us a little longer, while we explain.

A More Excellent Way

To coin a phrase from Scripture, "behold, I show you a more excellent way."

Anything would be "more excellent" than the way the Bible says things are going to be for unbelievers. The alternative to the end times holocausts is so pleasant and so simply attained that we feel we must say it one last time, complete with the method.

Believers, as we have seen, will see the rapture, the millennium, and eternity, rather than destruction and punishment. You can become a believer virtually at once.

The Lord's attitude on your salvation is clear: "I stand at the door and knock" (Revelation 3:20). "He is not willing that any should perish" (2 Peter 3:9). "As many as received him, to them gave he power to become the sons of God" (John 1:12).

Approaching God is quite a natural thing. He is, after all, the Creator of nature. There is hardly a thinking person anywhere who cannot see that nature has a Maker, and that the affairs of this world give the impression of having a plan. Supplied further with the truths of prophecy and the fact that they are coming out, the unbeliever can readily approach God without feeling strange.

You do not have to write or phone. God has indicated that He will hear you whatever your circumstances, wherever you are.

You do not have to be anybody special. Jesus had time for the lepers and thieves as well for as the mighty and powerful. You do not have to qualify in any special social group; the tax collectors and prostitutes go into heaven before the befrocked high priests of Israel, according to Jesus.

You do not have to change yourself over; God delights in taking care of that in return for your faith. You will be a happier, kinder, more loving individual, as you have always wanted to be, when Christ takes over your life.

And you will get the world's best "buyer protection plan." You will live on and on in joy and peace, avoiding the terrible ending of this world as we know it, and proceeding to the best of all possible worlds.

In talking to God, you should use your own words. He knows you, and there's no use putting up a false front.

You might try saying something on this order:

> Lord Jesus, I believe that You died for me and can give me everlasting life. Please do this for me and let me live for You from now on. Thanks.

Do it now. And we'll see you in the kingdom!

Moody Press, a ministry of the Moody Bible Institute, is designed for education, evangelization and edification. If we may assist you in knowing more about Christ and the Christian life, please write us without obligation to: Moody Press, c/o MLM, Chicago, Illinois 60610.